REAL ESTATE
ACCOUNTING MADE EASY

REAL ESTATE
ACCOUNTING MADE EASY

Obioma Anthony Ebisike

WILEY

John Wiley & Sons. Inc.

For general information on our other products and services, or technical support, please contact our Customer Care Department within the United States at 800-762-2974, outside the United States at 317-572-3993 or fax 317-572-4002.

Wiley also publishes its books in a variety of electronic formats. Some content that appears in print may not be available in electronic books.

For more information about Wiley products, visit our Web site at *http://www.wiley.com*.

ISBN: 978-0-470-60339-0; 978-0-470-64889-6 (ebk); 978-0-470-64891-9 (ebk); 978-0-470-64894-0 (ebk)

Printed in the United States of America

10 9 8 7 6 5 4 3 2 1

This book is dedicated to my parents, Richard and Josephine Ebisike, for giving me a wonderful life. I continue to admire the life they lived. They provided me and my siblings with a home and an atmosphere that inspires love, peace, and confidence. In so many ways they showed me the joy and power of a peaceful life.
I couldn't ask for a better home.

I am very grateful to my brother Sonny for giving me one of the first real opportunities to pursue my dreams. I am also very indebted to all my other brothers and sisters for their everlasting love and care. They helped in many ways by providing an arena in which I continue to strive for success and pursue my dreams. From birth they gave me love and care beyond any imagination. I am a product of their generosity. My life is full, and I feel rich just because of them.

I am also very grateful to all the members of Ebisike family. You are all a source of inspiration.

To all my teachers, I want to say thank you.

Contents

About the Author

Obioma Anthony Ebisike has over 10 years' work experience in accounting, in both the audit and real estate fields. He is currently a senior controller at a New York–based international real estate investment firm as well as an independent investor. Mr. Ebisike began his professional career at the New York office of Deloitte & Touche LLP, the international accounting firm, where he spent six years and rose to the position of audit and advisory services manager before leaving the public accounting sector.

While in the public accounting sector, Mr. Ebisike performed and managed client audits in numerous industries, such as real estate, consumer businesses, private equity, fund management, technology, media, telecommunication, public relations, and advertising, among others.

As part of his role in the real estate private sector, he has provided accounting training to his accounting and finance team and led discussions on the impact of emerging accounting rules and regulations.

Mr. Ebisike holds a bachelor's degree in accounting (magna cum laude) with minors in finance and economics, a master's degree in real estate finance and investments from New York University, and currently is pursuing a PhD in economics. He is also a Certified Public Accountant.

Mr. Ebisike is an avid reader and traveler and enjoys outdoor activities. He currently lives in New York City.

Preface

My goal in writing this book is twofold: to share with you my knowledge of the theories and practices of real estate from an accounting and financial perspective, and to provide a resource for easier understanding of the real estate industry from a financial standpoint. This book is a must-read for professionals and scholars interested in the real estate industry, especially investors, analysts, accountants, auditors, and students.

To make the subject easy to understand, the book starts from an introductory level; subsequent chapters build on the first few chapters.

The first two chapters introduce real estate terms and products and discuss basic real estate accounting. These chapters are fundamental to understanding the industry and gaining the most out of this book. They cover common terms used in the real estate industry as well as basic financial information common to the industry. Chapter 2 also covers basic accounting aspects of real estate transactions.

This book also introduces the reader to the different forms of entities in which real estate assets are held in Chapter 3. The discussion goes from the simplest form of real estate ownership—sole ownership—to partnerships, joint ventures, and real estate investment trusts (REITs). The characteristics as well as advantages and disadvantages of these forms of entities are discussed in detail.

Later chapters discuss the various aspects of real estate. Chapters 4 to 7 focus on the accounting for revenues, expenses, capital improvements and inducements, among other specific areas of transactions. There are in-depth discussions on budgeting, variance analysis, market research and analysis, valuation, and financing, which are covered in Chapters 8 to 12. Certain more complicated types of transactions, such as accounting for real estate investments, development costs, and percentage of completion revenue recognition, are also discussed in depth in Chapters 13 to 15. Chapter 16 discusses the various types of audits that real estate entities are subjected to. Audit processes and procedures are explained to help auditors, accountants, and management understand the roles and importance of audits. Common items normally requested by the auditors are also described.

I am confident that this book will further your understanding of the real estate industry. My hope in writing this book is that I am able to contribute to your understanding of this field.

Obioma Anthony Ebisike,
New York, New York

REAL ESTATE
ACCOUNTING MADE EASY

1

INTRODUCTION TO REAL ESTATE

Real estate is generally defined as land and all things that are permanently attached to it. These attachments include improvements made to add to the value of the land, such as irrigation systems, fence, roads, or buildings. When buyers purchase real estate, in addition to acquiring the physical land and its improvements, they acquire other specific rights related to that real estate. These rights include the right to control, exploit, develop, occupy, improve, pledge, lease, sell, or assign the real estate. These rights apply not only to the physical land and improvements but also to the ownership of all that are below and above the ground. These ownership rights normally can be separately leased or sold to interested parties; thus landowners can separately sell the space above a certain height on a particular piece of land. This space is normally called an air right. However, it is important to note that the use and transfer of air rights can be restricted or regulated by state and local laws.

TYPES OF REAL ESTATE ASSETS

Generally, a piece of land can be improved into different types of real estate assets. These improvements can be classified into seven different types of real estate:

1. Improved nonbuilt land
2. Residential properties
3. Commercial office properties
4. Industrial properties

5. Retail properties

6. Hotels

7. Mixed use properties

Improved Nonbuilt Land

In economics and business, land is described as one of the four factors of production. (The other factors include labor, capital, and entrepreneurship.) The value of land is derived from the demand for land for production of goods and also for the demand for goods and services created from improvements made to land. For example, the demand for rice requires the cultivation of the seed in farmland to grow the rice. Likewise, the demand for cars requires the need to build factories to produce the cars, and land is needed to build these factories. Therefore, even an empty land is an asset with measurable and in many cases significant value. Thus, a vacant land can be improved through proper irrigation and access roads for farming or with structures for the production of goods and services.

Residential Properties

Shelter is a basic necessity of life. In order to obtain it, residential properties must be constructed. The type of residential properties predominant in a particular area depends on factors such as availability of developable land, population and population growth, zoning laws, local government policies, and access to transportation, among others.

There are primarily four types of residential property:

1. Single-family and small multifamily properties

2. Garden apartment buildings

3. Mid-rise apartment buildings

4. High-rise apartment buildings

Single-Family and Small Multifamily Properties   Single-family residential properties are found mostly in suburban areas and usually are occupied by one family. Such houses normally would have a living room, bedrooms, kitchen, bathroom(s), and maybe a family room. They are usually occupied by the property's owner or rented out to a tenant. This type of residential property is not usually found in a central business district (CBD) because it requires more land space per family living unit than other types of residential properties, and they are usually more affordable in a suburban area.

A small multifamily residential property is similar to a single-family residential property but with more than one unit. Because of the multiple-unit structure, each unit is rented out to different individuals or families. These small multifamily properties can be between two and four separate units. In some cases the owner occupies one of the units and rents the other units to tenants. This type of residential property is also predominant in suburban areas and sometimes is also found in urban areas. In some cases it can be found near CBDs.

Garden Apartment Buildings   Garden apartment buildings usually are located in suburban areas and contain individual attached apartment units. They usually are built horizontally and normally are made up of three to four stories. In suburban areas, retirement homes and some condominiums and cooperative houses are built in this form. A typical garden apartment complex can have between 40 and 400 units. This type of residential property is more common in the suburbs because it requires significant land space due to the horizontal nature of the structures.

Mid-Rise Apartment Buildings   Mid-rise apartment buildings are more commonly found in urban areas. They are usually higher than 5 stories and can be up to 10 stories. In cities, mid-rise apartment buildings can be structured as condominiums and cooperatives properties. Unlike garden apartment complexes but similar to high-rise apartment buildings, mid-rise apartment buildings require relatively small land space. But the cost of land, even relatively small parcels, often is very expensive.

High-Rise Apartment Buildings   High-rise apartment buildings are usually towers built in urban areas. High-rise apartment buildings make effective use of the high cost of land in cities. High-rise buildings are usually taller than 11 stories. In major cities, such as London, New York, Tokyo, and Toronto, it is not uncommon to find 50-story high-rises. The construction costs of these towers are enormous. High-rises contain significant numbers of apartment units, certainly more than mid-rise apartment buildings.

Commercial Office Properties

Commercial office properties are properties constructed for commercial office activities. These properties can be found in both urban and suburban environments and are occupied by businesses for conducting business activities; however, they are predominantly found in CBDs. Office properties are usually classed either as A, B, or C. These classifications have no specific rules or criteria, and classifications in different cities vary; thus, what is classed as a Class A building in Dallas might have a different classification in Washington, D.C. However, some of the factors that affect a building's classification include amenities, type and condition of the elevator, lobby finishing, electrical and mechanical engineering efficiencies, adoption of modern energy concepts, design of the building, age, proximity to transportation, and tenant mix.

Generally, a Class A building is better in terms of the factors mentioned above than a Class B building in the same market. Class A buildings tend to be close to major transportation hubs; are new or relatively new, and have modern designs; have modern electrical and mechanical engineering systems; have modern heating, ventilation, and air-conditioning (HVAC) systems; and usually have major companies as tenants, among other attributes. Class B buildings tend to have fewer amenities than Class A buildings. They may have older electrical and mechanical systems and may be located farther away from main transportation hubs. Class B buildings also may have a mixture of major companies and less-known companies as tenants. Class C properties are much older buildings that have not undergone any major renovations for a long time. They also have older electrical and mechanical systems that lack current technological efficiencies. Most often Class C buildings are occupied by numerous, less-well-known companies with relatively small spaces rented to many tenants.

Industrial Properties

Industrial properties include manufacturing plants and warehouse facilities. These properties usually are built horizontally and are very large in size. Sometimes they are custom built to meet the specific needs of tenants due to the nature of the manufacturing process or the type of equipment used.

Industrial properties usually have simple structural designs with open space and very high ceilings. Some might have unique floor, wall, HVAC, or roofing specifications. The actual structure depends on the needs of the tenants. It is not unusual to find a manufacturing facility of up to 1 million square feet of horizontal space or a warehouse facility of the same size.

Industrial properties usually are located away from residential areas and urban cities. Due to amount of land required to construct these structures and also due to zoning restrictions, mostly they are located where land costs are relatively cheap. In some cases, the waste from these facilities can be unfit for normal living environments. In some areas, only certain locations far away from residential areas are zoned for industrial activities.

Retail Properties

Retail properties in general are built near residential neighborhoods and commercial districts. There are different types of retail properties; the most common types are:

- Convenience centers
- Neighborhood shopping centers
- Community shopping centers

- Regional shopping centers/malls
- Superregional shopping centers/malls
- Specialty centers
- Lifestyle centers
- Power centers
- Off-price outlets and discount centers/malls
- Strip commercial
- Highway commercial

The main differences among these types of retail properties are the size of the buildings and the nature and type of tenants. On one extreme are the convenience centers, which are usually less than 30,000 square feet; on the other extreme are the regional and superregional malls, which could be over 1 million square feet of shopping space. Exhibit 1.1 summarizes the attributes of each of these types of retail properties.

Exhibit 1.1 Types of Retail Properties

Type	Tenantry	Size	Trade Area
Convenience center	Stores that sell convenience goods (e.g., groceries, pharmaceutical); not anchored by a supermarket	Less than 30,000 sq. ft.	Less than 5-minute driving time
Neighborhood shopping center	Stores that sell convenience goods and stores that provide personal services (e.g., dry cleaning, shoe repair); a supermarket is often the principal tenant	30,000 to 150,000 sq. ft. of gross leasable area; 4 to 10 acres	Less than 5-minute driving time; 1 to $1\frac{1}{2}$ mile range; 5,000 to 40,000 potential customers
Community shopping center	Stores that sell convenience goods, personal services, and shopper goods (e.g., apparel, appliances); a junior department store or off-price/discount store is often the principal tenant; other	100,000 to 300,000 sq. ft. of gross leasable area; 10 to 30 acres (includes minimalls)	5- to 20-minute driving time; 3- to 6-mile range; 40,000 to 150,000 potential customers

(continued)

Exhibit 1.1 (Continued)

Type	Tenantry	Size	Trade Area
	tenants include variety or super-drugstores and home improvement centers		
Regional shopping center	Stores that sell general merchandise, shopper goods, and convenience goods; one or more department stores are the principal tenants	300,000 to 1,000,000 sq. ft. of gross leasable area; 30 acres; contains one or more department stores of at least 100,000 sq. ft.	20- to 40-minute driving time; 5- to 10-mile range; 150,000 to 400,000 potential customers
Superregional shopping center	Stores that sell general merchandise, apparel, furniture, home furnishings, and services as well as recreational facilities	Over 800,000 sq. ft. of gross leasable area; contains at least three major department stores of at least 100,000 sq. ft each	In excess of 30-minute driving time; typically 10- to 35-mile range; over 500,000 potential customers
Specialty, or theme center	Boutiques and stores that sell designer items, craft wares, and gourmet foods; a high-profile specialty shop is often the principal tenant; festival malls and fashion centers are types of theme centers	Same range as a neighborhood or community shopping center	Similar to that of a regional shopping center
Lifestyle centers	Stores that sell upscale home furnishing, women's fashion, department stores and restaurants	300,000 to 500,000	Similar to regional shopping center
Power center	A minimum of three, but usually five or more, anchor tenants that are dominant in their categories	Typically open-air centers of more than 250,000 sq. ft.; almost all space designed for large tenants	A minimum of 15 miles—typically a 20-minute range and a population of 400,000 to 500,000

Off-price outlet and discount center	Name-brand outlet stores and/or wholesales grocery and hadware stores	60,000 to 400,000 sq. ft.	Similar to superregional center
Strip commerical (a continuous row or strip along a main thoroughfare)	Convenience stores, fast-food restaurants, car dealerships, and service stations	Varies according to trade area	Neighborhood or community
Highway commercial	Motels, restaurants, truck stops, service stations; may stand as a single establishment within a cluster of other highway-related service facilities	Varies	Passing motorists in need of highway-related servies

Source: Stephen F. Fanning, *Market Analysis for Real Estate* (Chicago: Appraisal Institute, 2005), p. 192.

Hotels

There are numerous types of hotel properties, and they are classified based on the level of service, amenities, and size of the property. The four most common classifications are:

1. Full-service hotels

2. Boutique hotels

3. Extended-stay hotels

4. Motels

Full-Service Hotels   Full-service hotels provide guests with a variety of services, such as room service, restaurants on site, valet parking, spas, swimming pools, gymnastics centers, meeting rooms, and convention facilities. Some full-service hotels also have retail shopping and gift stores. Some examples of full-service hotels include Mandarin Oriental, Waldorf-Astoria, Marriott, and Hilton Hotels, among others. These hotels are usually big in size; some are 100,000 square feet or more. Many full-service hotels are well known due to their advertising budgets, services they provide, and amenities. In some cases these hotels are hotel franchises.

Boutique Hotels   Boutique hotels provide limited service compared to full-service hotels. They are mostly small in size and do not offer services such as convention facilities, restaurants, or room service or other amenities found at full-service hotels. Boutique hotels usually are less known and usually have smaller advertising budgets than full-service hotels.

Extended-Stay Hotels   Extended-stay hotels aim to be a home away from home. Each unit is designed with a larger room to feel homey, and they usually contain small kitchens complete with kitchen utensils. Customers often choose this type of hotel when they plan to stay for weeks or longer. Some examples include Hampton Inn & Suites, Embassy Suites, and Comfort Suites.

Motels   Motels are usually small lodging properties whose doors face a parking lot and/or common area with small rooms, with free parking targeting business travelers and tourists looking to spend a few nights. Motels offer very limited services; their rates usually are cheaper than all types of hotel accommodations. Most motels are located close to major highways and attraction centers. Motels usually do not provide services such as convention centers, spas, room service, or restaurants.

Mixed Use Properties

Mixed use properties are innovative concepts in real estate development. They contain a combination of two or more of the different types of properties mentioned earlier. Such properties can be hedges during down cycles in a particular real estate market. A mixed use property may have a residential component, a retail component, and a hotel component all in one. Some mixed use properties contain an office component, a retail component, and a hotel component. A mixed use property could be made up of any combination of the different types of real estate that is appropriate for that particular market. Mixed use has been very popular recently, especially in urban areas such as London, New York, Chicago, and Washington, DC, and Tokyo.

COMMON INDUSTRY TERMS

As we move from this introductory chapter of the book, we will encounter numerous new terms that are mostly familiar to professionals in real estate. To facilitate easier understanding for folks new to the industry, it is prudent to offer definitions of some common terms used by professionals in the real estate industry. Obviously this list is not all inclusive, but it is a great start to become familiar with the industry.

Accounting   The process of identifying, measuring, recording, classifying, summarizing, and communicating financial and economic transactions and events to enable users to make informed decisions.

Accounts Payable   A type of liability arising from the purchase of goods and services from suppliers or vendors on credit.

Accounts Receivable   A type of asset arising from the sale of goods and services to customers on credit.

Amortization   An accounting term used to describe the periodic writing off of an asset over a certain timeframe or the periodic repayment of a loan over a specified timeframe. Example: A landlord incurred $60,000 of attorney fees for drafting a tenant lease with a lease term of 5 years. Accounting principles require that the amount should be capitalized and amortized into expense over the lease term; thus, the monthly amortization expense would be ($60,000/60 months) $1,000.

Appraisal   An opinion about the market value of a property at a specific date. Appraisals usually are determined by licensed professionals.

Assets   In general, "probable future economic benefits obtained or controlled by a particular entity as a result of past transactions or events."[1] More simply, they can be thought of as properties and resources owned by an entity. Assets can be tangible such as land, buildings, furniture, and equipment or intangible such as acquired copyrights, trademarks, and patents. Assets are further classified as current or noncurrent depending on whether they can be converted into cash or used up within one year or one operating cycle, whichever is longer.

Balance Sheet   A financial statement that shows an entity's financial position at a point in time, such as at the end of a month, quarter, or year. A balance sheet has three main parts: assets, liabilities, and owners' equity. The components of these three main parts are listed on the balance sheet based on their relative liquidity. For example, cash balances are listed before accounts receivable, and accounts receivable are listed before inventories.

Bankruptcy   A term used to describe a party's inability to pay its liabilities as they become due. A bankruptcy is granted through a court proceeding and is filed under various bankruptcy codes, such as Chapters 7, 11, and 13. Each of these chapters has very different implications.

Budget   A formal plan set by management for forecasted business activities in future periods against which actual business activities would be evaluated. It enables the actual operations of an entity to be compared to management objectives.

---

1. Financial Accounting Standards Board, Statement of Financial Accounting Concepts No. 6, *Elements of Financial Statements* (Norwalk, CT: 1985), paragraph 25.

Capitalization Rate (Cap Rate)   The rate at which future cash flows are converted to a present value amount. This amount is usually expressed in percent. This rate is sometimes used in the valuation of real estate. A cap rate is commonly calculated using the formula:

$$\text{Cap Rate} = \text{Annual Net Operating Income/Cost (Purchase Price)}$$

Central Business District (CBD)   The central commercial and business center of a city. CBDs usually are where the major firms are located and are densely populated. CBDs usually are more accessible with better transportation systems than other parts of a city.

Condominium (Condo)   A collection of individual home units in which the units are owned individually but there is joint ownership of common areas and facilities. A residential condominium can be viewed as an apartment that the resident owns instead of rents. Usually there is no structural difference between a condominium and an apartment. Thus, by looking at a building you can't differentiate whether it is a condominium or apartment. The key difference between them is mostly the legal structure that defines a condominium as a form of ownership. Note also there are nonresidential condominiums as well, such as hotels, industrials, commercial, and retail condominiums.

Controller   An entity's chief accounting officer. The controller of an organization supervises the accounting, internal control, and financial reporting activities of an organization.

Cooperative Property (Co-op)   A property that is owned by a legal entity; each shareholder is granted the right to occupy one unit of the real estate. Shareholders pay rent to the corporation. They do not own the real estate but own shares of the real estate ownership entity.

CPA   Certified Public Accountant. A person holding this designation has passed a qualifying examination and met all the educational and work experience requirements of the profession to practice as a public accountant.

Creditor   An entity that is owed money.

Debt Coverage Ratio (DCR)   The ratio of net operating income (NOI) to the annual mortgage payment. This ratio is normally used in evaluating an entity's ability to fulfill its debt obligation.

Debtor   An entity that owes money to others.

Debt Service   The periodic repayment of a loan by the borrower to the lender. Periodic debt service may include only interest or could be interest and principal, depending on the loan agreement.

Deed   A written instrument that evidences the transfer of title from one party to another. The party transferring the title is called a grantor; the party receiving title is called the grantee.

Default   A party's failure to fulfill its obligation under any agreement. Examples include nonpayment or late payment of rent by a tenant, landlord's failure to provide agreed-upon services to the tenant, and debtor's failure to make agreed-on debt service payments.

Dividend   A return received by a shareholder on an investment. Dividends can be paid in the form of cash, shares, or properties. Dividends paid in the form of cash are referred to as cash dividends, dividends paid in the form of shares are referred to as share dividends, and those paid in the form of property are referred to as property dividends.

Effective Gross Income (EGI)   The expected rental income to be collected after adjusting for vacancies and reserves for uncollected rents.

Eminent Domain   The right of the government to take private property for public use upon payment of fair compensation to the owner. This right is regarded as the inherent right of the government. With this right the government can take over people's homes for purposes that qualify as public use.

Equity   Represents ownership interest in a real estate asset or securities. In real estate ownership financed with debt, the owner's equity is the difference between the real estate value and the loan balance.

Financing Costs   Costs incurred by a borrower in obtaining a loan. Examples of loan costs are application fees, origination fees, loan points, and filing fees.

Foreclosure   The legal process in which the mortgagee (lender) exercises its right under the loan agreement to force the sale of a mortgaged property upon a default by the mortgagor (borrower). A foreclosure proceeding is conducted through the legal system.

Fund from Operation (FFO)   A commonly used term by real estate investment trusts (REITs) to measure cash flow from the entity. It is also used as a measure of operating effectiveness of a REIT and regarded in the real estate industry as a better measure of performance than earnings. It is calculated as: net income plus depreciation and amortization minus gain from sales of real estate.

Future Value   The value in the future for funds deposited today. Example: The value one year from today of $905 deposited at a bank earning an interest rate of 10 percent is $1,000.

Gentrification   The remodeling of old homes to modern concepts and the conversion of properties from one use to another in a particular neighborhood. Examples include the conversion of rental apartments to condominiums, conversion of hotels to condominiums or to cooperative properties, or vice versa.

Gross Building Area (GBA)   The total area of all floors measured from the exterior of the building and including the superstructure and the substructure basement.

Gross Rentable Area (GRA)   The total floor area intended for tenants' occupancy and use. Basements, hallways, and stairways are included in this area.

Income Statement   Also called the statement of operation. Shows the financial performance of an entity over a period of time, such as during the month, quarter, or year.

Inflation   A general increase in the price level of goods and services in an economy. It is generally regarded as an erosion of the purchasing power of money. Inflation is normally expressed in percent per annum.

Inflation Risk   The risk that inflation will reduce the purchasing power of a certain amount of money over time.

Internal Rate of Return (IRR)   One of the measures of an investment's performance and is expressed as a percent. The inputs on an IRR calculation include the invested amount, the cash flows, and the reversion value. An IRR is sometimes described as the discount rate at which invested capital has a zero net present value.

Interest   Represents the cost of borrowed funds and is expressed in percent per annum. The amount paid for borrowed funds is called the interest cost, and the amount received for funds lent is called interest income.

Lease   A legal agreement between a lessor and a lessee that gives the lessee the exclusive right to use the lessor's property in return for rent for an agreed time period. A lease should, at a minimum, include the name of the parties, a description of the leased premises, terms of the lease, and the signature of the parties.

Lessee   The party that leases a property from another party. This party is usually the tenant. The lessee has the right to exclusive use of the property for an agreed-on period. The rights of the lessee are derived from the lease agreement and from the applicable law.

Lessor   The party that grants its exclusive right to use to another party. This is usually the landlord and owner of the leased property.

Liabilities   What an entity owes others. Liabilities can be classified as current or long-term liabilities. Current liabilities are those liabilities that are due within one year or one operating cycle, whichever is longer. Long-term liabilities are liabilities with due dates longer than one year or one operating cycle. Liabilities are listed on the balance sheet according to the due dates, with those due within the year or operating cycles listed first before, for example, those due in 10 years.

Loan Commitment Letter   Letter from a lender committing to provide a specific loan amount to a borrower for a specific purpose and for specified terms within a given period of time. A loan commitment letter can serve as evidence from a real estate purchaser to the seller of the purchaser's ability to close on the deal.

Loan-to-Value Ratio (LTV)   The ratio of the mortgage loan to the property's value.

Lien   The right to take and hold or sell the property of a debtor as security for a debt provided by a lender.

Mortgage   An instrument that evidences the lender's security interest in a debt-financed property.

Net Income   The net earnings of an entity over an accounting period. It is presented in an income statement and is determined by deducting all costs and expenses of the period from total income of the period.

Net Loss   The amount at which all costs and expenses of the period are higher than total income of the period. A net loss occurs when an entity is not profitable. It is basically the opposite of a net income and it is also presented in an income statement.

Net Operating Income (NOI)   The amount left after deducting operating expenses from gross income. This amount does not include depreciation, amortization, or debt service payments. NOI is widely used as a measure of operating profitability of a property.

Net Rentable Area (NRA)   The amount of space rented to a lessee, excluding the common areas of the property.

Present Value   The value today of a payment due in the future. Example: The value of $1,000 due 1 year from today discounted at the rate of 10 percent and compounded monthly is $905.

Prime Rate   The lowest interest rate that banks charge their best and largest customers on short-term borrowed funds.

Refinancing   The replacement of an old loan with a new loan by a borrower from the same or a different lender with more favorable loan terms.

Rent   The amount agreed between the lessee and lessor to be paid by the lessee in exchange for use of the lessor's premises. Rent can be expressed as a dollar amount or as dollars per square foot.

Retainage   In a construction project, represents a portion of the amount due under a construction contract that has not been paid by the owner to the contractor pending completion of the project in accordance with plans and specifications.

Retained Earnings   The accumulation of net earnings that were not distributed as dividends to the shareholders. Retained earnings are presented in a balance sheet and the statement of changes in shareholders' equity.

Secured Interest   A lender's interest on a mortgage used to finance the purchase or refinancing of an asset. A secured interest gives the lender the right to foreclose on the mortgage in the event of default by a borrower.

Securitization   The pooling of mortgages together and offering them as securities in the capital market. The underlying mortgaged properties therefore serve as collateral for these securities.

Statement of Cash Flows   A financial statement that shows how cash came in and went out of an entity during an accounting period.

Statement of Changes in Shareholders' Equity   A financial statement that presents a summary of all transactions that affected equity during an accounting period. In a sole proprietorship, this is referred to as the statement of changes in owner's equity.

Time Value of Money   The concept that $1 today is worth more than $1 in the future because of the interest factor since if you deposit $1 today in a bank, that $1 will earn interest over time.

Title   A term commonly used to link the owner(s) of a real estate to the real estate itself. It is the bundle of rights that the real estate owner(s) have in the real estate. In some cases this term is also used to refer to the legal document that evidences ownership of real estate.

Title Insurance   A type of insurance that protects the holder of a title against claims to the title or obtaining bad title in a transaction.

Townhouse   A single-family residential property that is attached to another property, usually another townhouse. Each unit is separately owned.

Underwriting   The process undertaken by a lender to decide whether credit should be extended based on the creditworthiness of the borrower and the condition and value of the property to be used as collateral.

Workout   The various action plans agreed to between a defaulted debtor and creditor(s). A workout agreement details the rights and obligations of each party necessary to enable the creditor(s) to get full or partial refund of their loan to the debtor.

Zoning   Restrictions by the government on land use. With zoning, the government regulates the type of buildings that can be developed in certain areas. Example: Some areas can be zoned for residential, commercial, industrial, or mixed use. Zoning can also be used to restrict the height of buildings in a given geographic area.

2

BASIC REAL ESTATE ACCOUNTING

The term "accounting" refers to the process of identifying, measuring, recording, classifying, summarizing, and communicating financial transactions and events to enable users to make informed decisions. Users of accounting information include business managers, analysts, business owners, creditors, regulators, investors, customers, and suppliers, among others. The wide range of users of accounting information underscores the importance of accounting knowledge in business. No one can run a very successful business today without a basic understanding of accounting or the advice of an accountant. Accounting information is not used only by for-profit organizations; it is also very useful in nonprofit organizations.

HISTORY OF DOUBLE-ENTRY BOOKKEEPING

An important aspect of accounting is its double-entry bookkeeping system. This system was first publicized by Italian mathematician Luca Pacioli in his 1494 book, *Summa de arithmetic, geometric, proportion et proportionality*, and is widely regarded as the first published treatise on bookkeeping as we know it today. However, the earliest known uses of double-entry bookkeeping date back to the Farolfi ledger around 1299s, used by the Italian merchant named Giovanno Farolfi & Company, and also the use of double-entry bookkeeping by the Treasurer's accounts of the city of Genoa in Italy in 1340. The principle of this system is that business transactions are best recorded in accounts, and each transaction should be recorded in at least two accounts with at least one credit and one debit going to each of the accounts. The total credits must equal the total debits. This mechanism was meant to serve as a recording error self-check on the transactions.

TYPES OF ACCOUNTS

An account is a location within an accounting system in which the debit and credit entries are recorded. Organizations use numerous types of accounts in recording transactions. These accounts are grouped into eight categories.

1. Assets

2. Liabilities

3. Owner's equity

4. Revenues

5. Expenses

6. Gains

7. Losses

8. Extraordinary items

Asset Accounts

The term "assets" was defined by the Financial Accounting Standards Board (FASB)[1] as probable future economic benefits obtained or controlled by a particular entity as a result of past transactions or events. Assets represent properties and resources owned by an entity.

Examples of asset accounts are:

- Cash and cash equivalents

- Investments: stocks, bonds, certificates of deposit

- Accounts receivable

- Notes receivable

- Prepaid assets: prepaid insurance, prepaid rent, prepaid taxes

- Property, plant, and equipment

- Furniture

- Land

- Buildings

- Inventories

---

1. Financial Accounting Standards Board, Statement of Financial Accounting Concepts No. 6, *Elements of Financial Statement* (Norwalk, CT: 1985), paragraph 25.

Liabilities Accounts

The FASB defines "liabilities" as probable future sacrifices of economic benefits arising from present obligations of a particular entity to transfer assets or provide services to other entities in the future as a result of past transactions or events. "Liability" can also simply be described as what an entity owes others.

Examples of liabilities are:

- Accounts payable to vendors
- Salaries and wages payable to employees
- Taxes payable to the government
- Notes and loans payable to lenders
- Unearned revenues

Equity Accounts

Equity represents the entity owners' net stake in the business entity. The term "owner's equity" is commonly used in a sole proprietorship form of business. If the entity is a corporation, the term "stockholders equity" is commonly used; in a partnership, such equity is commonly referred to "partnership interest."

Mathematically,

$$Equity = Assets - Liabilities$$

This means that if you deduct the total liabilities of an entity from its total assets, the remainder is the owners' equity in the business.

A typical equity section of a corporation would have these accounts:

- Common stock at par value
- Common stock: additional paid-in capital
- Preferred stock
- Treasury stock
- Retained earnings

Not every entity has all these equity subaccounts. Some entities may have just common stock at par value, paid-in capital, and retained earnings.

A sole proprietorship will have a capital account only for the sole owner; a partnership may list the capital account of each of the partners.

Revenue Accounts

An entity's revenue represents inflow of assets received in exchange for goods or services provided to customers as part of the major or central operations of the business.[2]

Common revenue accounts in a real estate operation include:

- Base rents
- Operating expenses recoveries
- Property taxes recoveries
- Percentage rents from tenants
- Antenna rents

Other asset inflows that entities normally have separate accounts for include interest income and vending machine income.

Expenses Accounts

Expenses are outflows or the using up of assets as a result of the major or central operations of a business.[3]

Common expense accounts in a real estate operation include:

- Salaries and wages
- Electricity
- Cleaning
- Taxes
- Management fees
- Security
- Insurance
- Water and sewer
- Repairs and maintenance
- General and administrative expenses

Gain Accounts

Gains represent the excess amounts received or receivable for assets sold above their book values. They can also include increases in fair

---

2. Ibid., paragraph 78.
3. Ibid., paragraph 80.

market value of investments above their purchase prices. Examples of gains include:

- Realized and unrealized gains on marketable securities
- Gains on sale of equipment
- Gains on sale of land
- Gains on sale of buildings

Loss Accounts

Losses represent amounts at which amounts received or receivable from sale of assets are less than the book values of the assets. They can also include decreases in fair market value of investments below their purchase prices. Examples of losses include:

- Realized and unrealized losses on marketable securities
- Losses from sale of equipment
- Losses from sale of land
- Losses from sale of buildings

Note that, in practice, companies might have one or a few accounts to record both the gains and losses from the transactions mentioned in the gains and losses sections.

Extraordinary Items

The "Extraordinary Items" account is used to record transactions that are infrequent and unusual to the entity. Some examples of extraordinary items may include:

- Gain or loss from disposal of a business unit
- Casualty loss from fire accident not covered by insurance
- Certain effects of change in accounting methods

Note, however, that due to the nature of the entity, the examples given here might not be recorded as extraordinary items if they are not infrequent or not unusual to the entity.

ACCOUNTING METHODS

There are two principal methods in which business transactions can be recorded in an entity's accounting system: cash basis and accrual basis.

Cash Basis

Cash basis accounting is a method of bookkeeping in which revenues are recognized when the related cash is received and expenses are recorded when cash is paid. This method is commonly used in small businesses where transactions are less complicated and where revenues are mostly cash sales and purchases are mostly cash purchases. Usually, when this method is used, accounts receivable, accounts payable, and prepaid expenses are very immaterial to the business entity.

Accrual Basis Accounting

Accrual basis accounting is based on two very important accounting principles: the revenue recognition principle and the matching principle. The revenue recognition principle says, among other things, that revenues should be recognized at the time they are earned, not when cash is received; the matching principle says that expenses should be recorded in the same accounting periods as the revenues are earned as a result of the expenses incurred.

The U.S. generally accepted accounting principles (GAAP) and federal tax and the International Financial Reporting Standard all require all financial statements to be prepared under the accrual basis of accounting.

In the United States, there are two main methods of the accrual basis: GAAP basis and federal tax basis. Both require the use of the accrual method of accounting. Although the accrual method used is similar, there are certain areas in which transactions are treated differently. A few common examples are presented next.

Rental Revenue Recognition   According to Financial Accounting Standard 13, paragraph 19(b), GAAP requires that rent should be recognized as income over the lease term on a straight-line basis unless another systematic and rational basis is more representative of the time pattern in which the leased property is used, in which case that basis should be used. In practice, the use of another method other than straight-lining is very rare for entities using the GAAP basis accounting. However, the federal tax code requires rental revenue to be recognized when earned and due from the tenant, although if Internal Revenue Code, Section 467, is applicable, the rental revenue should be straight-lined.

Depreciable Life   Under GAAP, capitalized assets are depreciated over their useful life; however, under the federal tax basis, different classes of assets have specified depreciable uses. For example, under GAAP, buildings are depreciated over 40 years, while under the federal tax basis, they are depreciated over 30 years with exemption to 40 years if the entity has tax-exempt partner(s).

Reserve for Doubtful Receivables   Under GAAP, receivables deemed to be uncollectible are reserved and recorded with a debt to bad debt expense and a credit entry to a contra accounts receivable account. If the receivable is subsequently collected, the entry would then be reversed. However, under a federal tax basis, receivables are written off only when all efforts to collect have been exhausted and uncollectibility is determined. No reserve is allowed, only a write-off of the receivable.

Prepaid Rent from Tenants   Under GAAP, rents are recognized over the lease term on a straight-line basis. However, on a federal tax basis, rent received in advance is recorded as revenue in the period it is received.

RECORDING OF BUSINESS TRANSACTIONS IN THE ACCOUNTING SYSTEM

Before journal entries are recorded, accountants should have evidence to support the transactions to be recorded. This evidence, in the form of source documents, ensures that the journal entries and subsequent financial reports are accurate and can stand the test of time. It also enables the entity to pass any subsequent audits of its internal controls and financials.

Source documents serve as the evidence and support for the recording of business transactions and should be obtained before entries are recorded. They should also be retained for a reasonable period of time based on the nature of the transactions.

Some common examples of source documents in a real estate entity include:

- Purchase orders
- Vendor invoices
- Bills to tenants
- Employee time sheets
- Payroll records
- Bank statements
- Canceled checks
- Mortgage statements
- Lease agreements
- Vendor contracts

JOURNAL ENTRIES

After the source documents are received and the proper approvals for the transactions are obtained, the journal entries should be recorded. Obtaining approval for the transaction is very important because it ensures the validity of the transaction. For example, companies require every vendor invoice received to be reviewed and approved by a manager before the invoice is recorded or paid. This is a very useful control because it ensures the accuracy of information in the accounting system.

Some common examples of journal entries using the double-entry bookkeeping system are shown next.

Revenue Recognition Journal Entries

(i)	Cash	$10,000	
	Rental Revenue		$10,000
	(To recognize rental revenue and collection of the cash)		
(ii)	Accounts Receivable	$10,000	
	Rental Revenue		$10,000
	(To recognize rental revenue and receivable from the tenant)		
(iii)	Cash	$10,000	
	Accounts Receivable		$10,000
	(To record collection of cash received from tenant for receivable recorded in journal entry ii)		
(iv)	Cash	$1,000	
	Interest Income		$1,000
	(To record interest income on cash at the bank)		

Expenses Journal Entries

(i)	Salaries Expenses	$5,000	
	Cash		$5,000
	(To record payment of salaries to employees)		

At some companies, employees may not be paid just at the end of the month. For instance, some companies pay their employees every two weeks. To ensure that salary expenses are recorded in the correct period, an accrual would need to be recorded at the end of the accounting period with this journal entry (assume amount due at the end of period is $3,500):

(ii)	Salaries Expense	$3,500	
	Accrued Expenses		$3,500
(iii)	Utility Expense	$1,000	
	Cash or Accounts Payable		$1,000
	(To record utilities expense for the period)		
(iv)	Cleaning Expense	$1,000	
	Cash or Accounts Payable		$1,000
	(To record cleaning costs for the period)		

Journal entries similar to these should be recorded for all expenses incurred during an accounting period.

Depreciation Expenses   Assets acquired by an entity with more than one year of useful life are required to be capitalized and depreciated over their useful lives. Examples of these types of assets include buildings, equipment, mechanical and electrical systems, and furniture. It is important to note that land is not a depreciable item in accounting.

Assume an entity purchased a building for $5 million. Of that amount, $1 million represents the value of land. The remaining $4 million ($5m – $1m) would need to be depreciated over the building's useful life, usually 40 years.

The annual depreciation expense based on this information would be:

Purchase price	$5,000,000
Allocation to land	$1,000,000
Allocation to building improvement	$4,000,000
Depreciable life (yr)	40
Annual depreciation	$400,000

The annual depreciation journal entry would be:

Depreciation Expense	$400,000	
Accumulated Depreciation		$400,000

Prepaid Expenses Journal Entries   Prepaid assets or expenses are assets or expenses paid for in advance of their use or prior to the period in which the expenses are incurred. Examples include prepaid insurance, prepaid taxes, and prepaid leasing costs.

Let us assume that on December 20, 2008, an entity paid $120,000 for 12 months of property insurance for the period January 1, 2009 through December 31, 2009. The prorated monthly cost of the insurance would be ($120,000/12 months) $10,000.

Therefore, the journal entry to be recorded for this transaction on December 20, 2008, when the payment was made, would be:

Prepaid Insurance	$120,000	
Cash		$120,000

At the end of each month starting on January 31, 2009, the entity would need to record this journal entry to recognize each month's insurance expense and reduce the prepaid insurance:

Insurance Expense	$10,000	
Prepaid Insurance		$10,000

Therefore, on January 31, 2009, the prepaid insurance account would have a balance of $110,000, which is determined as:

Original Prepaid Insurance on 12/20/08	$120,000
January 2009 Insurance Expense	10,000
Prepaid Insurance Balance on 1/30/09	$110,000

BASIC ACCOUNTING REPORTS

A collection of all of an entity's accounts with their individual balances is referred to as the general ledger. Thus, a general ledger contains all the journal entries recorded with the respective debits and credits.

In some cases financial information users might be interested in just the ending balance of each account for a particular period instead of the details. This information can be obtained in a report called the trial balance, which is a summary of all accounts with their respective balances.

The information from a trial balance can be summarized and presented in an even more condensed form called financial statements. These statements show the entity's financial position and performance both at a point in time and over a period of time. The four main types of financial statements are:

1. Income statement

2. Balance sheet

3. Statement of changes in shareholders' equity

4. Statement of cash flows

Income Statement

The income statement is also called the statement of operations. It shows the financial performance of an entity over a period of time. The period could be for a week, month, quarter, or year. An income statement shows whether the entity earned a profit or incurred a loss during the period. This is indicated as net income or net loss on an income statement.

Some of the common line items that are found in an income statement include:

- Revenues
- Expenses
- Gains

- Losses
- Extraordinary items
- Net Income

Exhibit 2.1 shows the income statement of Boston Properties for the year ended December 31, 2007.

Balance Sheet

A balance sheet is a financial statement that shows an entity's financial position at a point in time, such as at the end of a month, quarter, or year. A balance sheet is also referred to as a statement of financial position. The balance sheet shows the assets, liabilities, and shareholders' equity at a particular date. Five of the line items commonly found in a balance sheet include:

1. Current assets
2. Long-term assets
3. Current liabilities
4. Long-term liabilities
5. Equity section

Current Assets   Current assets consist of:

- Cash and cash equivalents
- Accounts receivable
- Short-term investments: stocks, bonds, and certificates of deposit (CDs)
- Short-term notes receivable
- Prepaid assets

Long-term Assets   Long-term assets consist of:

- Equipment
- Land
- Buildings
- Intangible assets

Exhibit 2.1 Boston Properties, Inc. Consolidated Statements of Operation

	For the Year Ended December 31,		
	2007	2006	2005
	(In thousands, except for per share amounts)		
Revenue			
Rental:			
Base rent	$ 1,084,308	$ 1,092,545	$ 1,098,444
Recoveries from tenants	184,929	178,491	170,232
Parking and other	64,982	57,080	55,252
Total rental revenue	1,334,219	1,328,116	1,323,928
Hotel revenue	37,811	33,014	29,650
Development and management services	20,553	19,820	17,310
Interest and other	89,706	36,677	11,978
Total revenue	1,482,289	1,417,627	1,382,866
Expenses			
Operating			
Rental	455,840	437,705	434,353
Hotel	27,765	24,966	22,776
General and administrative	69,882	59,375	55,471
Interest	285,887	298,260	308,091
Depreciation and amortization	286,030	270,562	260,979
Losses from early extinguishments of debt	3,417	32,143	12,896
Total expenses	1,128,821	1,123,011	1,094,566
Income before minority interests in property partnerships, income from unconsolidated joint ventures, minority interest in Operating Partnership, gains on sales of real estate and other assets, discontinued operations and cumulative effect of a change in accounting principle	353,468	294,616	288,300
Minority interests in property partnerships	(84)	2,013	6,017
Income from unconsolidated joint ventures	20,428	24,507	4,829

Income before minority interest in Operating Partnership, gains on sales of real estate and other assets, discontinued operations, and cumulative effect of a change in accounting principle	373,812	321,136	299,146
Minority interest in Operating Partnership	(64,916)	(69,999)	(71,498)
Income before gains on sales of real estate and other assets, discontinued operations and cumulative effect of a change in accounting principle	308,896	251,137	227,648
Gains on sales of real estate and other assets, net of minority interest	789,238	606,394	151,884
Income before discontinued operations and cumulative effect of a change in accounting principle	1,098,134	857,531	379,532
Discontinued operations:			
Income from discontinued operations, net of minority interest	6,206	16,104	15,327
Gains on sales of real estate from discontinued operations, net of minority interest	220,350	—	47,656
Income before cumulative effect of a change in accounting principle	1,324,690	873,635	442,515
Cumulative effect of a change in accounting principle, net of minority interest	—	—	(4,223)
Net income available to common shareholders	$ 1,324,690	$ 873,635	$ 438,292
Basic earnings per common share:			
Income available to common shareholders before discontinued operations and cumulative effect of a change in accounting principle	$ 9.20	$ 7.48	$ 3.41
Discontinued operations, net of minority interest	1.91	0.14	0.57
Cumulative effect of a change in accounting principle, net of minority interest	—	—	(0.04)
Net income available to common shareholders	$ 11.11	$ 7.62	$ 3.94
Weighted average number of common shares outstanding	118,839	114,721	111,274
Diluted earnings per common share:			
Income available to common shareholders before discontinued operations and cumulative effect of a change in accounting principle	$ 9.06	$ 7.32	$ 3.35
Discontinued operations, net of minority interest	1.88	0.14	0.55
Cumulative effect of a change in accounting principle, net of minority interest	—	—	(0.04)
Net income available to common shareholders	$ 10.94	$ 7.46	$ 3.86
Weighted average number of common and common equivalent shares outstanding	120,780	117,077	113,559

Current Liabilities   Current liabilities consist of:

- Accounts payable
- Salaries payable
- Taxes payable
- Short-term debts
- Unearned revenues

Long-term Liabilities   Long-term liabilities consist of:

- Loans
- Other long-term liabilities

Equity Section   The equity section consists of:

- Common stocks
- Additional paid-in capital
- Retained earnings
- Treasury stock

In a balance sheet, the total of an entity's assets must equal the sum of liabilities and equity, thus the formula:

$$Assets = Liabilities + Equity$$

Exhibit 2.2 shows the balance sheet of Boston Properties, Inc. as of December 31, 2007.

Exhibit 2.2   Boston Properties, Inc. Balance Sheet (in thousands, except for share and par value amounts)

	December 31, 2007	December 31, 2006
ASSETS		
Real estate, at cost:	$ 10,249,895	$ 9,552,458
Less: accumulated depreciation	(1,531,707)	(1,392,055)
Total real estate	8,718,188	8,160,403
Cash and cash equivalents	1,506,921	725,788
Cash held in escrows	186,839	25,784
Investment in securities	22,584	—
Tenant and other receivables (net of allowance for doubtful accounts of $1,901 and $2,682, respectively)	58,074	57,052

Accrued rental income (net of allowance of $829 and $783, respectively)	300,594	327,337
Deferred charges, net	287,199	274,079
Prepaid expenses and other assets	30,566	40,868
Investments in unconsolidated joint ventures	81,672	83,711
Total assets	$ 11,192,637	$ 9,695,022

LIABILITIES AND STOCKHOLDERS' EQUITY

Liabilities:

Mortgage notes payable	$ 2,726,127	$ 2,679,462
Unsecured senior notes (net of discount of $3,087 and $3,525, respectively)	1,471,913	1,471,475
Unsecured exchangeable senior notes (net of discount of $18,374 and $0, respectively)	1,294,126	450,000
Unsecured line of credit	—	—
Accounts payable and accrued expenses	145,692	102,934
Dividends and distributions payable	944,870	857,892
Accrued interest payable	54,487	47,441
Other liabilities	232,705	239,084
Total liabilities	6,869,920	5,848,288
Commitments and contingencies	—	—
Minority interests	653,892	623,508

Stockholders' equity:

Excess stock, $.01 par value, 150,000,000 shares authorized, none issued or outstanding	—	—
Preferred stock, $.01 par value, 50,000,000 shares authorized, none issued or outstanding	—	—
Common stock, $.01 par value, 250,000,000 shares authorized, 119,581,385 and 117,582,442 issued and 119,502,485 and 117,503,542 outstanding in 2007 and 2006, respectively	1,195	1,175
Additional paid-in capital	3,305,219	3,119,941
Earnings in excess of dividends	394,324	108,155
Treasury common stock at cost, 78,900 shares in 2007 and 2006	(2,722)	(2,722)
Accumulated other comprehensive loss	(29,191)	(3,323)
Total stockholders' equity	3,668,825	3,223,226
Total liabilities and stockholders' equity	$ 11,192,637	$ 9,695,022

Statement of Changes in Shareholders' Equity

In a sole proprietorship, the statement of changes in shareholders' equity is called statement of changes in owners' equity.

This statement presents a summary of all transactions that affected equity during an accounting period. As mentioned, the period could be during the month, quarter, or year.

The statement starts with the beginning equity balance, then presents the changes that occurred during the accounting period, and concludes with the ending equity balance. Examples of transactions that can affect share-holders' equity include:

- Net income or loss during the period
- Issuance of new shares
- Buyback of outstanding share (treasury stock)
- Declaration of dividends
- Other comprehensive income and losses

See Exhibit 2.3 for the statement of changes in shareholders' equity of Boston Properties, Inc. for 2007.

Statement of Cash Flows

A statement of cash flows shows how cash came into the entity and how cash left the entity during an accounting period. It basically shows cash inflows and outflows. The ending cash balance on a statement of cash flows also agrees to the cash balance at the end of the period that is reported on the balance sheet.

A statement of cash flows is broken out into three sections, namely:

1. Cash flows from operating activities
2. Cash flows from investing activities
3. Cash flows from financing activities

Cash Flows from Operating Activities   This section of the statement of cash flows shows cash inflows and outflows from the entity's operating activities. Common cash inflows include:

- Cash received from tenants
- Receipt of accounts receivable
- Cash received for interest income

Common cash outflows include:

- Cash paid for current period operating expenses
- Cash paid for liabilities from prior period for operating expenses
- Cash paid for interest expenses

The cash flow from operating activities section can be reported in one of two different ways: the direct or the indirect method. Under the direct

Exhibit 2.3 Boston Properties, Inc. Statement of Stockholders' Equity (in thousands)

	Common Stock		Additional Paid-in Capital	Earnings in Excess of Dividends	Treasury Stock, at Cost	Unearned Compensation	Accumulated Other Comprehensive Loss	Total
	Shares	Amount						
Stockholders' Equity, December 31, 2004	110,320	$1,103	$2,633,980	$325,452	$(2,722)	$(6,103)	$(15,637)	$2,936,073
Reclassification upon the adoption of SFAS No. 123R			(6,103)			6,103	—	—
Conversion of operating partnership units to Common Stock	925	9	59,915					59,924
Allocation of minority interest			8,163					8,163
Net income for the year				438,292				438,292
Dividends declared				(581,639)				(581,639)
Shares issued pursuant to stock purchase plan	8		424					424
Net activity from stock option and incentive plan	1,289	13	49,340					49,353
Effective portion of interest rate contracts							6,058	6,058
Amortization of interest rate contracts							698	698
Stockholders' Equity, December 31, 2005	112,542	1,125	2,745,719	182,105	(2,722)	—	(8,881)	2,917,346
Conversion of operating partnership units to Common Stock	3,162	32	287,321					287,353
Allocation of minority interest			20,020					20,020
Net income for the year				873,635				873,635
Dividends declared				(947,585)				(947,585)
Shares issued pursuant to stock purchase plan	8		526					526
Net activity from stock option and incentive plan	1,791	18	66,355					66,373
Effective portion of interest rate contracts							4,860	4,860
Amortization of interest rate contracts							698	698
Stockholders' Equity, December 31, 2006	117,503	1,175	3,119,941	108,155	(2,722)	—	(3,323)	3,223,226
Conversion of operating partnership units to Common Stock	1,342	13	143,297					143,310
Allocation of minority interest			15,844					15,844
Net income for the year				1,324,690				1,324,690
Dividends declared				(1,038,521)				(1,038,521)
Net activity from stock purchase plan	6		1,241					1,241
Net activity from stock option and incentive plan	651	7	24,896					24,903
Effective portion of interest rate contracts							(25,656)	(25,656)
Amortization of interest rate contracts							(212)	(212)
Stockholders' Equity, December 31, 2007	119,502	$1,195	$3,305,219	$394,324	$(2,722)	$—	$(29,191)	$3,668,825

method, the net operating cash balance is determined by tracking all individual cash receipts and cash disbursements during the period. However, under the indirect method, the net income is adjusted noncash items, such as depreciation and amortization expenses and other noncash expenses. In addition, the net income is also adjusted for increases and decreases in certain balance sheet items that affected cash during the period but did not affect net income for the period. Some of these accounts include but are not limited to accounts receivables, accounts payables, prepaid expenses, and liability accounts.

Cash Flows from Investing Activities   This section of the statement of cash flow shows cash inflows and outflows from an entity's investment activities. Common examples of cash inflows are:

- Proceeds from sale of investments in stocks, bonds, and CDs
- Proceeds from sale of property, plant, and equipment
- Collection of principal on loans to others
- Proceeds from sale of investments in unconsolidated joint ventures

Common examples of cash outflows are:

- Cash paid for investment in stocks, bonds, and CDs
- Cash paid for purchase of property, plant, and equipment
- Loans and notes to other entities
- Investments in unconsolidated joint ventures

Cash Flows from Financing Activities   This section of the statement of cash flow shows cash inflows and outflows related to debt financing as well as transactions with shareholders. Some common cash inflows are:

- Cash received for issuance of new shares
- Cash received for issuance of bonds and notes

Some common cash outflows are:

- Cash paid to buy back shares (treasury stock)
- Cash dividend to shareholders
- Repayment of bonds and notes

See Exhibit 2.4 for the statements of cash flows of Boston Properties, Inc.

Exhibit 2.4 Boston Properties, Inc. Consolidated Statements of Cash Flows

	For the Year Ended December 31,		
	2007	2006	2005
		(in thousands)	
Cash flows from operating activities:			
Net income available to common shareholders	$ 1,324,690	$ 873,635	$ 438,292
Adjustments to reconcile net income available to common shareholders to net cash provided by operating activities:			
Depreciation and amortization	288,978	276,759	267,641
Non-cash portion of interest expense	9,397	7,111	5,370
Non-cash compensation expense	12,358	8,578	7,389
Minority interest in property partnerships	84	(2,013)	(6,017)
Distributions (earnings) in excess of earnings (distributions) from unconsolidated joint ventures	(13,271)	(16,302)	2,350
Minority interest in Operating Partnership	245,700	186,408	113,738
Gains on sales of real estate and other assets	(1,189,304)	(719,826)	(239,624)
Losses from early extinguishments of debt	838	31,877	2,042
Loss from investment in unconsolidated joint venture	—	—	342
Cumulative effect of a change in accounting principle	—	—	5,043
Change in assets and liabilities:			
Cash held in escrows	(2,564)	(166)	(3,828)
Tenant and other receivables, net	(1,341)	(7,051)	(31,378)
Accrued rental income, net	(38,303)	(53,989)	(64,742)
Prepaid expenses and other assets	10,686	4,319	2,011
Accounts payable and accrued expenses	3,833	(2,502)	4,148
Accrued interest payable	7,046	(470)	(2,759)
			(continued)

35

Exhibit 2.4 (Continued)

	For the Year Ended December 31,		
	2007	**2006**	**2005**
		(in thousands)	
Other liabilities	5,318	(9,735)	9,305
Tenant leasing costs	(34,767)	(48,654)	(37,074)
Total adjustments	(695,312)	(345,656)	33,957
Net cash provided by operating activities	629,378	527,979	472,249
Cash flows from investing activities:			
Acquisitions/additions to real estate	(1,132,594)	(642,024)	(394,757)
Investments in securities	(22,584)	(282,764)	(37,500)
Proceeds from sale of securities	—	—	37,500
Net investments in unconsolidated joint ventures	(7,790)	23,566	2,313
Cash recorded upon consolidation	3,232	—	—
Net proceeds from the sale/financing of real estate placed in escrow	(161,321)	(872,063)	—
Net proceeds from the sale of real estate released from escrow	—	872,063	—
Net proceeds from the sales of real estate and other assets	1,897,988	1,130,978	749,049
Net cash provided by investing activities	576,931	229,756	356,605

3

FORMS OF REAL ESTATE ORGANIZATIONS

Real estate ventures are organized in numerous forms. This chapter explores these forms and presents an in-depth analysis of the characteristics of each form.

The form of ownership of a real estate venture is very important because it has a direct impact on the nature and extent of risks assumed and tax benefits and burdens applicable to the business entity. The ownership structure also impacts the extent of control by investors. Investors have choices on the form of ownership structure to hold their real estate investments. If an investor wants to go it alone, he or she can acquire property under his or her name, which is the most common in the acquisition of a primary residence. But when real estate acquired is for investment purposes, investors are better served when they use the other forms of ownership structure. The seven most widely used forms of real estate ownership are:

1. Sole ownership

2. Common and joint ownership

3. Partnership

4. Joint venture

5. Corporation

6. Limited liability company

7. Real estate investment trust (REIT)

SOLE OWNERSHIP

Sole ownership occurs when ownership is in the name of one individual. This is one of the most common forms of ownership of primary residences and small multifamily residential real estate properties. An investment property can also be held through sole ownership; however, one disadvantage of this form of ownership is that unlike some other forms, the investor has unlimited liability above and beyond the amount of the investment such that if there is a lawsuit related to the ownership of the property that requires financial damages to be paid to a plaintiff, the investor could be personally liable for such damages. In a sole ownership, all tax benefits and burdens of the acquisition, operation, and disposition of the real estate fall directly on the individual. Income generated by the real estate will be added to the investor's other incomes and taxed accordingly. Deductions generated by the real estate, subject to various loss limitations, such as the at-risk rules and the passive loss rules, will reduce the individual's income subject to tax.[1] There is no double taxation. This form of ownership can offer the best tax advantage; it is also the simplest form of ownership structure. Investors can protect themselves from the unlimited liabilities nature of this form of ownership by obtaining adequate liability insurance and using proper and adequate real estate management practices.

COMMON AND JOINT OWNERSHIP

Common and joint ownerships are unincorporated forms of ownership in which title is held by two or more investors. In this type of ownership structure, the business is controlled by the individual investors. This form of ownership has all the advantages and disadvantages of sole ownership. The owners have undivided interest in the business venture.

Some forms of this type of ownership are structured as common ownership; others are structured as joint ownership. An owner in a common ownership is called a tenant in common; an owner in a joint ownership is called a joint tenant. Though common and joint ownership are very similar, there are two very important differences between them:

1. In a common ownership, each owner can sell, pledge, or will his or her ownership interest with the permission of the other co-owners; in a joint ownership, no owner can sell, pledge, or transfer his or her interest.

---

1. F. David Windish, *Real Estate Taxation* (Chicago: CCH Inc., 2005), p. 42.

2. In a joint ownership, there is the right of survivorship. This means that if one of the owners dies, the surviving owner becomes the sole owner of all the interest in the real estate business. In a common ownership there is no right of survivorship, thus, if one of the owners dies, the ownership interest will go to the dead owner's heir(s). Because in the United States the laws vary in each state with regard to the characteristics of common and joint ownership, it is important to consult an attorney when setting up this type of ownership.

Apart from common and joint ownership, there is a similar third type of unincorporated ownership called tenancy by the entirety. This is available only to married couples, and ownership is treated as if the couple were a single individual. In some states in the United States, the same right is given to domestic partners as well.

PARTNERSHIPS

Instead of going it alone in a real estate venture as a sole owner, an investor might decide to collaborate with one or more additional investors in the business venture. By partnering with these additional investors, the business would have far more resources available to it.

A partnership is an unincorporated entity under state statutes and common law in the United States and does not have any specific statutory law governing it in the U.S. federal government. It is, however, formed by the partnership agreement of the partners. This agreement governs the relationship between the partners and the management of the partnership. This form of ownership is defined by the Uniform Partnership Act (UPA) as "an association of two or more persons to carry on as co-owners a business for profit." As stated in the definition, to qualify as a partnership, the association has to be a business carried out for profit. The owners of a partnership are called partners; their partnership interests do not have to be equal. Each partner's ownership interest is based on the agreement of the partners. Another important point noted by the UPA definition is that the partnership is an association of "persons." "Persons" here mean individuals, other partnerships, corporations, limited liability companies, real estate investment trusts, or joint ventures.

Reason for Partnerships

One of the major reasons investors use the partnership form of business is that it allows two or more persons to pool their resources together while still achieving the same economic and tax benefits available to a sole owner. Partnership formation is also relatively easy and costs less than forming and registering a corporation or other forms of ownership.

Legal Characteristics of a Partnership

1. A partnership must have two or more persons who are co-owners.

2. The purpose of the association should be for a business engaged for profit.

3. There should be an agreement between the partners; it can be expressed or implied.

Types of Partnerships

There are two main types of partnership. Each has unique attributes that differentiates it from the other form. The two types of partnerships are general and limited.

General Partnership   General partnership is a type of partnership in which all partners have equal rights in the partnership and are jointly and severally liable for the liability of the partnership. The owners of a general partnership are called general partners. Six common characteristics of a general partnership are:

1. There is mutual agency relationship. This means that every general partner is an agent of both the partnership and every other partner.[2] Therefore, the partnership will be held responsible for agreement with third parties signed by any of the partners on behalf of the partnership that are within apparent capacity of the partner.

2. Management of the partnership is vested with the general partners, and they all have equal right to bind the partnership.

3. The partners' liability to creditors is unlimited and is jointly and severally among the partners. Thus a creditor can go after any of the partners personally if the partnership is unable to pay its debts.

4. Unless the partnership agreement says otherwise, a simple majority vote of the partners is required in cases when the partners cannot agree unanimously.

5. A general partnership is not subject to income taxes but is required to file an information return with the applicable state and federal tax authorities.

6. The partnership may be dissolved on the occurrence of certain events, such as the bankruptcy of any of the partners, death of a partner, and withdrawal of a partner, among others, as agreed to by the partners in the partnership agreement.

---

2. Haried, Imdieke, Smith, *Advanced Accounting* (New York: John Wiley & Sons, Inc., 1994).

Limited Partnership   A limited partnership is defined as a partnership with one or more general partners and one or more additional partners whose liabilities are limited to their contribution to the partnership. The partners with limited liabilities are called limited partners; they do not get involved in the management of the partnership. Any limited partners who perform activities that are deemed to involve management of the partnership may lose their limited liability privileges.

Four characteristics of a limited partnership are:

1. There should be at least one general partner and one limited partner.

2. The liabilities of the limited partners are limited to their contribution to the partnership, unless the limited partner is deemed to be involved with management of the partnership.

3. Management of the partnership should be the responsibility of the general partner(s). The responsibilities of a general partner in both a general partnership and a limited partnership are the same.

4. A. limited partnership must file and record a certificate of limited partnership with state authorities where the business is located in order to obtain limited liability protection for the limited partners.

JOINT VENTURES

A joint venture is an arrangement among two or more parties, generally governed by a written agreement signed by all the parties, to carry out one project or transactions or a series of related transactions over a short period of time for the mutual benefit of the group. Joint ventures are commonly organized as a general or limited partnership or as a limited liability company.

The three main characteristics of a joint venture are:

1. There are at least two parties to the agreement.

2. The purpose of the arrangement is for one project or for a limited purpose that is for mutual benefit of the parties to the arrangement.

3. A joint venture may be organized for any number of reasons, not just to make a profit for the group members. It could be for social, recreational, research, or educational purposes.

CORPORATIONS

A corporation is a legal entity, separate from its owners and chartered under a state or federal law. Equity ownerships in a corporation are broken into units called shares, and the owners are called shareholders. Shareholders of a corporation have limited liability up to amounts invested in the corporation.

A corporation can be publicly or privately (closed) held. A public corporation is a corporation whose shares are traded through any of the stock exchanges, such as the New York Stock Exchange, Nasdaq, American Stock Exchange, London stock exchange, and others. Privately held stocks are not traded in an exchange but can be sold through private transactions.

As mentioned, corporations are separate legal entities and are therefore taxed separately from their shareholders. Corporations are further classified into two kinds based on their income tax treatment: C corporations and S corporations.

C Corporations

C corporations are generally referred to as regular corporations. They are taxed as separate legal entities and therefore separately from the shareholders. One of the disadvantages of a C corporation is double taxation. "Double taxation" means that the corporate earnings are taxed at the corporation level, and dividends received by shareholders are also taxed as income to them.

S Corporations

Although S corporations are legal entities separate from their shareholders, they do not pay taxes. In an S corporation, only the dividends received by the shareholders are taxed. Unanimous consent of the shareholders is required to form an S corporation, and the corporation must file documents with the taxing authorities.

A C corporation can elect to be treated as an S corporation if the corporation meets four requirements:

1. The corporation does not have more than 100 shareholders.

2. The corporation must have only one class of shares.

3. All shareholders must be U.S. citizens or residents and are individuals; however, certain tax-exempt organizations are allowed.

4. Entities electing S corporation status must be domestic corporations or limited liability companies.

It is important to note that if the corporation at any time fails to meet these four criteria, the election terminates. In addition, the S corporation status may also terminate if 25 percent or more of the S corporation's gross receipts for three years came from passive investment income and the S corporation also has calculated earnings not distributed to the shareholders.

Characteristics of a Corporation

C and S corporations have these seven characteristics:

1. They are separate legal entities from the shareholders.

2. C corporations are subject to income taxes at the corporate level while S corporations are not. However, dividends to shareholders from both C and S corporations are included by shareholders as income and therefore taxed.

3. Shareholders of both C and S corporations elect the board of directors, which in turn appoints the management that runs the day-to-day operations of the corporation.

4. Shareholders' liabilities are limited to the capital contribution to the corporation unless in cases where there is piercing of the corporate veil. Piercing of corporate veil is a legal action in which the shareholders and directors are made personally responsible for the liabilities of the company.

5. Equity ownerships are broken out into units called shares.

6. Corporations may have infinite life.

7. Both C and S corporations are subject to property, payroll, sales, and use taxes similar to other forms of business.

LIMITED LIABILITY COMPANIES

Limited liability companies (LLCs) have characteristics that are found in S corporations and partnerships. These features have made LLCs a very attractive form of ownership in various industries, including real estate. An LLC combines features from S corporations, such as limited liability of the investors, with some features from partnerships, such as exemption from income taxes. LLCs are usually structured to be taxed as partnerships; thus, they are required to pay income taxes not at the corporation level but at the individual investor level.

Owners of an LLC are called members. LLC can be run by managers elected from among the members of the LLC or hired by the members.

Six major characteristics of limited liability companies are listed next.

1. A member's liability is limited to his or her capital contribution, similar to limited partners in a limited partnership and shareholders in a corporation.

2. Management of the LLC may be members or individuals hired by the members.

3. There is no limit on the number of members.

4. Unlike an S corporation, there is no limitation on the kind of investors.

5. The LLC can issue different classes of shares.

6. LLCs can be structured to be classified as partnerships for federal income tax purposes.

REAL ESTATE INVESTMENT TRUSTS

Real estate investment trusts (REITs) were created by Congress in 1960 as an investment vehicle through the Real Estate Investment Trust Act. This act authorized a real estate structure in which taxes are levied only at the individual shareholder level instead of both at the corporate and shareholder level, as in some other corporate entities. The REIT ownership structure gives investors the ability to participate in the ownership of major real estate assets in the marketplace. "REITs offer all investors, not just the big players, a liquid way to invest in a diversified portfolio of commercial properties."[3] This means that through REITs, small investors with just a few hundred dollars can own a portion of prime real estate assets by purchasing shares of a REIT that owns the properties.

There are many different types of REITs, and REITs can be classified based on whether they are publicly traded or privately owned. In addition, they can be classified based on the type of assets held, such as residential, office, industrial, hotel, healthcare, diversified, or retail; thus, there are residential property REITs, office property REITs, industrial property REITs, and so on.

REITs have unique characteristics that differentiate them from other forms of real estate entities. These four characteristics are mandated by the Real Estate Investment Act and are discussed next.

1. Ownership composition

2. REIT assets

3. Income source

4. Distribution of income

Ownership Composition

The Real Estate Investment Act requires that for an entity to qualify as a REIT, there have to be no fewer than 100 investors. In addition, no fewer

---

3. David Geltner, Norman G. Miller, Jim Clayton, and Piet Eichholtz, *Commercial Real Estate Analysis & Investment*, 2nd ed. (Mason, OH: Thomson Higher Education, 2007), p. 586.

than 5 investors can own more than 50 percent of the entity. Through this act, Congress tried to ensure that the benefits of REITs are made available to a larger population of ordinary investors in the market.

REIT Assets

The purpose of a REIT is for investment in the real estate industry. To prevent this investment structure from abuse, the act requires that at least 75 percent of a REIT's total assets must be invested in real estate, mortgages secured by real estate, cash, or treasury securities.

Income Source

Not only should 75 percent of a REIT entity's assets be invested in real estate, mortgage, cash, or treasury securities; 75 percent of the entity's annual gross income should come primarily from rents and mortgage interests. This requirement again is to ensure that the REIT invests in real estate and other related assets.

Distribution of Income

Although one of the main goals of the REIT structure is to encourage investment in real estate, Congress also made sure that the government still receives its tax revenues. Congress achieved this by requiring that for an entity to retain its REIT status, the entity must pay at least 90 percent of its taxable income each year to the shareholders so that the shareholders can pay their share of the tax obligation.

4

ACCOUNTING FOR OPERATING PROPERTY REVENUES

In general, properties derive revenues through multiple channels. Some of these include base rent, operating expenses recoveries, real estate taxes recoveries, bill-back profits, antenna space rental, operation of vending machines, among others. In most cases, agreements called leases govern the relationships between the landlord and tenants. Therefore, a lease can be defined as an agreement between the landlord and tenant for the rental of the landlord's premises to the tenant for specified terms and conditions.

The lease can be short term or long term. Short-term leases are normally for one year or less; long-term leases are usually for more than one year. Most residential leases tend to be short term. Commercial office leases tend to be long term due to the need to stabilize the revenue stream of the property and also due to the high cost of finalizing a lease, which normally includes significant costs on broker's commissions, attorney fees, and document preparation, including time involved in the potential tenants' viewing the premises and negotiating the lease. Typically, leasing costs on commercial space are paid by the landlord; however, the attorney hired by the tenant is paid by the tenant. A typical long-term lease could range from 5 years to 15 years, depending on the market.

TYPES OF LEASES

In practice, there are multiple leasing arrangements between landlords and tenants. Four such arrangements include:

1. Gross lease
2. Net lease

3. Fixed base lease

4. Base-year lease

Each of these lease arrangements determines which party bears the risk of future operating cost increases and to what extent.

Gross Lease

A gross lease is a type of lease arrangement in which the tenant pays a specified amount that covers the rental of the premises, including the operating expenses and real estate taxes of the property. In this type of lease, the tenant's future total rental payments are known from day 1, and the landlord bears the risk of future operating expenses and real estate tax increases. Some tenants prefer this type of lease arrangement because it helps them manage the risk of future cost increases and planning.

Example

Union Plaza LLC, the owner of Union Plaza, a 45-story office building in downtown Boston, rents a 10,000-square-foot space to APB Dental Services ("tenant"). The lease is for five years, and tenant will pay the landlord the following rental to cover rental of the premises, which includes all operating expenses and real estate taxes of the premises:

Year 1	$100,000
Year 2	$100,000
Year 3	$105,000
Year 4	$110,000
Year 5	$115,000

Under this simplified example, the listed amounts are the full and only rental payments due to the landlord from this tenant during the lease period. The tenant does not pay any additional amount in respect to operating expenses and taxes. Whether the cost of operating the building goes up or down in the future will not have an impact on the amounts noted.

Net Lease

In a net lease arrangement, the tenant pays a minimum base rent in addition to the tenant's proportionate share of operating expenses and real estate taxes. In this type of lease, the landlord recovers from the tenant operating costs and real estate taxes. This arrangement is also referred to as triple net or net net net lease.

Example

Western 465 Tower LLC, the owner of a property located at 465 Tower Lane in Boston, is leasing the whole fifteenth floor of the 25-story property to Ashwood & Brown Partners LLC ("tenant"), a prestigious hedge fund that is currently located two blocks from the property. The lease specifies that for the 10-year lease, Ashwood & Brown would pay a minimum base rent as indicated in addition to its pro rata share of the property. The minimum base rents are:

Years	Rent per Square Foot
1	$80.00
2	$82.00
3	$84.00
4	$86.00
5	$88.00
6	$90.00
7	$92.00
8	$94.00
9	$96.00
10	$98.00

The fifteenth-floor space to be leased to Ashwood & Brown has a total net rentable area (NRA) of 30,000 square feet. The entire building has a total NRA of 600,000 square feet. The parties remeasured the space and agreed on the sizes listed, noting that the tenant's pro rata share is 5 percent of the building. This amount would be used in determining the tenant's share of operating expenses and real estate taxes.

In determining the tenant's share of operating expenses and real estate taxes, let us assume that the total operating expenses in year 1 are $15,247,000 and real estate taxes are $4,435,000. Therefore, the additional rent would be:

Operating expenses	$15,247,000
Real estate taxes	$4,425,000
	$19,672,000
Ashwood & Brown pro rata share	5%
Ashwood & Brown additional rent—Yr 1	$983,600

Note that in most cases, the parties would agree that the tenant would pay monthly the minimum base rent plus its estimated monthly pro rata share of operating expenses. For real estate taxes, the tenant would pay its share of the taxes based on when they are due to the government taxing authority. (Tax due dates vary depending on the municipality.)

Therefore, excluding the real estate taxes, the tenant's total monthly payment for the first year of the lease would be determined in this way:

(continued)

(continued)
    Step 1. Calculate the monthly minimum base rent.

Monthly Minimum Base Rent:

Minimum annual base rent (80 per square foot × 30,000)	$2,400,000
Number of months	12%
Monthly minimum base rent	$200,000

Step 2. Calculate the estimated monthly operating expenses.

Estimated Monthly Operating Expenses:

Estimated year 1 annual operating expenses	$15,247,000
Tenant pro rata share percent	5%
Tenant pro rata annual share	$762,350
Estimated monthly operating expenses	$63,529

Step 3. Add the monthly minimum base rent and the estimated monthly operating expenses.

Monthly minimum base rent	$200,000
Estimated monthly operating expenses	$63,529
Tenant's total monthly rent payment	$263,529

Since the operating expenses paid by the tenant each month is an estimated amount, at the end of each year, the landlord would have to perform a reconciliation of the actual operating expenses incurred in running the property and compare that to the estimate paid by the tenants during the course of the year to determine if additional rent is due from the tenant or if a refund is due to the tenants. The lease normally would indicate the timeframe when this reconciliation would need to be finalized by the landlord and communicated to the tenant. Some leases also give the tenants an audit right. An audit right is the tenant's right under the lease to review the books and records of the landlord to ensure that the amounts are appropriately included or excluded as operating expenses of the property.

Fixed Base Lease

The fixed base lease is a hybrid of a gross lease and net lease. In a fixed base lease, the tenant pays a gross amount that covers the base rental of the premises plus operating expenses. However, the total amount that the tenant pays is broken down into the base rental and the operating expenses. At the end of the year, if the tenant's pro rata share of actual operating expenses is greater than the operating expenses portion of the amount included in the gross payments paid by the tenant over the course of the year, the landlord would bill the tenant for the additional amount. If, however, the tenant's pro rata share of the actual operating expenses is less than the operating expenses portion of the gross payment, the tenant does not get a credit or refund.

Example

A landlord and tenant agree that tenant pays $100.00 per square foot (psf) for 10,000 square feet of space of an office building under a fixed base lease arrangement. The parties agree that $40.00 of the $100.00 represent the operating expenses of the property. At the end of year 1 of the lease, the landlord performed a reconciliation of the operating expenses incurred on the building. The total expenses were determined to be $47.00 psf.

In this case since actual operating expenses ($47.00) are greater than the amount of estimated operating expenses ($40.00) by $7.00, the landlord would bill the tenant for an additional rent of $70,000. This additional rent is determined as:

Actual year 1 operating expenses	$47.00
Operating expenses in estimated gross payment	$40.00
Difference	$7.00
Net rentable area (NRA)	10,000
Additional rent due from tenant	$70,000.00

If the actual operating expenses after the reconciliation show operating expenses as $38.00 psf, the total rent paid by the tenant would remain $100.00 psf without any year-end adjustments.

Base-Year Lease

The year in which a lease started is called the base year of a base-year lease. During the base year, tenants pay a whole amount that represents the rental of the premises plus the tenants' pro rata share of operating expenses during that year. In subsequent years, if the operating expenses are greater than the operating expenses incurred during the base year, the landlord is entitled to bill tenants their pro rata share of the increase over the base-year operating expenses.

Example

AB Realty is the owner of a 10-story, 100,000-square-foot office property of which 10,000 square feet was rented to Watson & Associates LLP under a base-year lease arrangement. The lease started in 2009 for a 5-year lease term. The parties agreed to a total rent of $100.00 psf based on 2009 operating expenses of $2,300,000.

(continued)

(continued)

In 2010 the tenant continues to pay $100.00 psf as agreed to in the lease. However, the total operating expenses for 2010 were $3,050,000, which is an increase of ($3,050,000 – $2,300,000) $750,000 from the base-year operating expenses.

If AB Realty's pro rata share of operating expenses is 10 percent of total operating expenses for each year of the lease, then AB Realty would have to pay the landlord an additional rent of $75,000. This amount is calculated as:

Total 2010 operating expenses	$3,050,000
Minus base-year operating expenses	$2,300,000
Increase over base-year operating expenses	$750,000
Multiply by tenant pro rata share	10%
Additional rent due	$75,000

Note, however, that if the 2010 operating expenses had been less than the base-year operating expenses, the tenant would not have been entitled to any refund or credit.

REVENUE RECOGNITION

According to Securities and Exchange Commission's Staff Accounting Bulletin (SAB) 104, in general, revenue should be recognized when it is realized or realizable and earned; and revenue is deemed realized or realizable and earned when these four criteria are met:

1. Persuasive evidence of an arrangement exists.

2. Delivery has occurred or services have been rendered.

3. The seller's price to the buyer is fixed or determinable.

4. Collectibility is reasonably assured.

SAB 104 recognizes that the accounting literature on revenue recognition practices includes broad conceptual discussions as well as certain industry-specific guidance. It therefore allows for the use of any specific authoritative literature if such transaction is within its scope. Thus, the four criteria can be utilized where there is no industry-specific guidance. The principal accounting guidance for real estate revenue recognition is Financial Accounting Standard No.13 and its subsequent amendments. Financial Accounting Standard No. 13, Financial Accounting Standard No. 29, Financial Accounting Standard No. 98, FASB Technical Bulletin 85-3, FASB Technical Bulletin 88-1, SAB 101, and SAB 104 are among the important accounting literatures that provide guidance on accounting for real estate revenue recognition.

This chapter simplifies these accounting pronouncements for ease of use.

LEASE CLASSIFICATION

Leases are classified from the point of view of the lessee or lessor. Therefore, they should be accounted for differently based on specific criteria and aspects of the lease. These criteria determine how the lease transaction is recorded on the books of both the lessee and the lessor.

There are two lease classifications: lessee lease classification and lessor lease classification.

Lessee Lease Classification

From the point of view of the lessee, leases are classified into two categories: operating leases and capital leases.

Lessor Lease Classification

From the point of view of the lessee, leases are classified into these categories:

- Operating leases
- Sales-type leases
- Direct financing leases
- Leverage leases

Generally, in practice, the operating lease is the most common type of lease; thus it is the focus of this chapter. The main difference between an operating lease and the other types of leases is that no asset or liability is recorded at the inception of an operating lease by the lessee based on the current accounting guidance. However, for the other types, the lessee records an asset and liability equal to the present value of the minimum lease payments over the lease term.

Financial Accounting Standard No. 13, paragraph 5, presents some very important terms useful for proper understanding of the accounting guidance on lease transactions.

> *Inception of a lease.* [T]he date of the lease agreement or commitment, if earlier. For purposes of this definition, a commitment shall be in writing, signed by the parties in interest to the transaction, and shall specifically set forth the principal terms of the transaction. However, if the property covered by the lease has yet to be constructed or has not been acquired by the lessor at the date of the lease agreement or commitment, the inception of the lease

shall be the date that construction of the property is completed or the property is acquired by the lessor.

Bargain purchase option. A provision allowing the lessee, at his option, to purchase the leased property for a price which is sufficiently lower than the expected fair value of the property at the date the option becomes exercisable that exercise of the option appears, at the inception of the lease, to be reasonably assured.

Bargain renewal option. A provision allowing the lessee, at his option, to renew the lease for a rental sufficiently lower than the fair rental of the property at the date the option becomes exercisable that exercise of the option appears, at the inception of the lease, to be reasonably assured.

Lease term. The fixed non-cancelable term of the lease plus (i) all periods, if any, covered by bargain renewal options . . . , (ii) all periods, if any, for which failure to renew the lease imposes a penalty on the lessee in an amount such that renewal appears, at the inception of the lease, to be reasonably assured, (iii) all periods, if any, covered by ordinary renewal options during which a guarantee by the lessee of the lessor's debt related to the leased property is expected to be in effect, (iv) all periods, if any, covered by ordinary renewal options preceding the date as of which a bargain purchase option is exercisable, and (v) all periods, if any, representing renewals or extensions of the lease at the lessor's option; however, in no case shall the lease term extend beyond the date a bargain purchase option becomes exercisable. A lease which is cancelable (i) only upon the occurrence of some remote contingency, (ii) only with the permission of the lessor, (iii) only if the lessee enters into a new lease with the same lessor, or (iv) only upon payment by the lessee of a penalty in an amount such that continuation of the lease appears, at inception, reasonably assured shall be considered "noncancelable" for purposes of this definition.

Minimum lease payments.

i. *From the standpoint of the lessee.* The payments that the lessee is obligated to make or can be required to make in connection with the leased property. However, a guarantee by the lessee of the lessor's debt and the lessee's obligation to pay (apart from the rental payments) executory costs such as insurance, maintenance, and taxes in connection with the leased property shall be excluded. If the lease contains a bargain purchase option, only the minimum rental payments over the lease term and the payment called for by the bargain purchase option shall be included in the minimum lease payments. Otherwise, minimum lease payments include the following:

a. The minimum rental payments called for by the lease over the lease term.

b. Any guarantee by the lessee of the residual value at the expiration of the lease term, whether or not payment of the guarantee constitutes a purchase of the leased property. When the lessor has the right to require the lessee to purchase the property at termination of the lease for a certain or determinable amount, that amount shall be considered a lessee guarantee. When the lessee agrees to make up any deficiency below a stated amount in the lessor's realization of the residual value, the guarantee to be included in the minimum lease payments shall be the stated amount, rather than an estimate of the deficiency to be made up.

   c. Any payment that the lessee must make or can be required to make upon failure to renew or extend the lease at the expiration of the lease term, whether or not the payment would constitute a purchase of the leased property. In this connection, it should be noted that the definition of lease term (defined above) includes "all periods, if any, for which failure to renew the lease imposes a penalty on the lessee in an amount such that renewal appears, at the inception of the lease, to be reasonably assured." If the lease term has been extended because of that provision, the related penalty shall not be included in minimum lease payments.

  ii. *From the standpoint of the lessor.* The payments described in (i) above plus any guarantee of the residual value or of rental payments beyond the lease term by a third party unrelated to either the lessee or the lessor, provided the third party is financially capable of discharging the obligations that may arise from the guarantee.

    Initial direct costs. Those incremental direct costs incurred by the lessor in negotiating and consummating leasing transactions (e.g., commissions and legal fees).

These definitions are very important in understanding a lease and properly recording the related accounting transaction, especially in relation to rental revenue straight-lining.

ADDITIONAL COST RECOVERIES

Apart from minimum rental payments by the tenant for the use of the landlord's premises, additional costs are incurred by the landlord in operating the building. These costs are in one way or another recovered by the landlord from the tenants. Some examples of these recoveries are:

- Real estate taxes
- Cleaning services
- Security services

- Repairs and maintenance
- Utilities
- Heating, ventilation, and air conditioning
- Management fees
- Freight services

Except for real estate taxes, in most cases these recoveries are paid monthly to the landlord. Real estate taxes are treated differently because the frequency of payment depends on when they are due to the taxing authority where the property is located. In some localities they are due monthly; in others they could be due quarterly, semiannually, or annually. Therefore, tenants prefer paying based on when the real estate taxes are due to the authorities.

OPERATING EXPENSES GROSS-UP

Operating expenses gross-up is a lease clause that helps landlords adequately recover certain variable operating expenses due to building vacancies. It allows the landlord to adjust upward certain variable and semivariable operating expenses to what they could have been if the building was fully occupied. This clause applies only when a building's occupancy is less than the lease definition of full occupancy.

The lease normally contains the parties' definition of "full occupancy," as this may not always mean 100 percent occupancy. For the purpose of calculation of gross-up, the parties may agree that when the property is 95 percent occupied, it should be deemed as fully occupied.

To help explain further how gross-up is calculated, let us use a simple example. An office property is 87 percent occupied throughout the year. Actual operating expenses subject to gross-up are $550,000, of which $100,000 represents the fixed portion of the operating expenses; thus, $450,000 is subject to gross-up. Assume per the lease that 95 percent is defined as full occupancy of the property. Therefore, the total recoverable expenses after gross-up would be determined as:

Steps	Description	Amount
1	Operating Expenses incurred and to be grossed-up (includes fixed and variable components)	$550,000
2	Minus Fixed Component of Expense	100,000
3	Variable Component of Expense	$450,000
4	Divide by Weighted Average Occupancy (WAO) during the Year	87%
5	Variable Expense	517,241

6	Multiply by Full Occupancy as Defined by Lease (%)	95%
7	Grossed-up Variable Expense	491,379
8	Plus Fixed Component of Expense (from above)	100,000
9	**Total Grossed-up Expense**	**$591,379**

To determine each tenant's share of the recovery, the tenant's pro rata share would be multiplied by the total grossed-up cost of $591,379. Note also that some tenants' leases might specify that the landlord may not recover more than 100 percent of the amount actually paid for operating expenses; this stipulation has to be considered in determining the recoveries from the tenants.

CONTINGENT RENTS

Contingent rents are additional rents to the landlord that can materialize when certain agreed-on thresholds are met. This type of arrangement is commonly found in retail leases. A typical contingent rent entitles the landlord, in addition to other rental payments already discussed, to a percentage of the retail tenant's sales after a certain amount. This arrangement can be beneficial to the landlord and the tenant, depending on the final sales number. To the tenant, it allows for a higher rent only if there is an increase in sales. It allows the landlord to share in the success of the tenant.

Example

Island Strip Mall LLC leased a 5,000-square-foot space to Berney Retail Stores for 10 years. The parties agreed that the rent would be $25.00 psf with an increase of 3 percent annually plus the tenant's pro rata share of operating expenses and real estate taxes. In addition, the tenant is to pay the landlord 5 percent of the tenant's annual gross sales over $2,000,000.

Assume at the end of the first year of the lease, the tenant's gross sales are $3,000,000. Contingent revenue to the landlord for the first year of the lease would be $50,000. This amount is calculated as:

Tenant's first-year sales	$3,000,000
Sales threshold	$2,000,000
Sales above threshold	$1,000,000
Rate	5%
Contingent revenue due to the landlord	$50,000

The landlord should recognize the contingent revenue only at the point when the threshold has been met. Thus, in the example, the landlord cannot recognize any contingent revenue until the tenant's gross sales have reached $2,000,000. This accounting is based on the interpretation of SEC SAB 101,

(continued)

(continued)

Revenue Recognition in Financial Statements. Note also that Emerging Issue Task Force (EITF) 98-8, which deals with lessee accounting of contingent rental expense, is silent on the accounting by the lessor. However, the author of this book believes that the accounting of contingent revenue by the landlord just described is consistent with accounting for contingencies.

EITF, however, requires that a lessee should recognize contingent rental expenses over the measurement period even though the actual amount to be recognized can be precisely determined only toward the latter part of the measurement period or at the end of the accounting period. Therefore, lessees should take care in forecasting the sales amount used in determining contingent rental expenses.

RENT STRAIGHT-LINING

In practice, the total rental payment to the lessor from the lessee is comprised mostly of the minimum lease payments, operating expenses and real estate tax recoveries, and contingent rentals. As was described earlier, the minimum lease payments can be agreed by the lessor and lessee to increase by a certain agreed amount through the lease term. In most cases the parties can agree that the increase would be based on certain external factors such as the Consumer Price Index (CPI).

For U.S. generally accepted accounting principles (GAAP) reporting, FAS 13 requires that rent shall be recognized on a straight-line basis over the lease term unless any other "systematic and rational basis is more representative of the time pattern in which users benefit from the leased property."

This particular area of lease accounting has generated a lot of confusion related to such questions as what portion of the rent should be straight-lined and when straight-lining should start and end in cases where there are free rents and bargain renewal options, among other questions. These questions are answered here.

FASB Technical Bulletin 85-3 explains FAS 13 further by saying that

> . . . scheduled rent increases, which are included in minimum lease payment under Statement 13, should be recognized by lessors and lessees on a straight-line basis over the lease term unless another systematic and rational allocation basis is more representative of the time pattern in which the leased property is physically employed *Accounting for Operating Leases with Scheduled Rent Increases*, Norwalk, CT: 1985]

An important comment to note in this statement that relates to the first question raised above is what portion of the rent should be straight-lined. Only the minimum lease payment should be straight-lined. Exclude from the straight-line schedule operating expenses recoveries, real estate tax recoveries, and contingent rents because these amounts cannot be determined at the inception of the lease for the whole lease term. Note that an exception is in gross lease arrangements; in those cases, the minimum lease payments already include the tenant's portion of operating expenses and real estate taxes.

Rent straight-lining should start on the lease inception date regardless of whether there are free rents given to the lessee at the beginning of the lease term. This lease start date for the purpose of rent straight-lining should be the tenant's beneficial occupancy date. Also, the straight-lining should end on the lease expiration date. However, there are a few exceptions. One exception is on a GAAP basis reporting where payments from the landlord are to be accounted for as tenant improvements and the tenant was granted access to the leased space prior to the substantial completion of the improvement. In this case the straight-lining may not start on the beneficial occupancy date. This topic is discussed more fully in Chapter 7. Another exception is where the lease contains a bargain renewal option. As described earlier, a bargain renewal option gives the lessee the right to renew the lease at a significantly lower rental rate. There is a presumption here that the lessee would renew the lease, thereby extending the lease term. Therefore, in a lease with a bargain renewal option, the straight-lining should be extended to assume that the lease would be renewed by the lessee.

Example

To illustrate rent straight-lining, a 400,000-square-foot four-story office property with five tenants is 100 percent occupied and has these leases.

1. Roxy Clothing is retail tenant and occupies 40,000 square feet of space on the first floor of the property. The lease is for 5 years with inception date of July 1, 2009 and 6 months free rent. The lease is also a gross lease. A breakdown of the tenant's rent is:

Rent Start Date	Rent End Date	Rent
July 1, 2009	December 31, 2009	$ —
January 1, 2010	December 31, 2010	$3,200,000
January 1, 2011	December 31, 2011	$3,500,000
January 1, 2012	December 31, 2012	$3,800,000
January 1, 2013	December 31, 2013	$4,100,000
January 1, 2014	June 30, 2014	$2,200,000

The tenant has no renewal option right; however, the landlord is entitled to receive 3 percent of gross sales after sales of $15,500,000. Actual gross sales for 2009 and 2010 were $10,000,000 and $22,000,000 respectively.

(continued)

(continued)

2. ABC Grocery Store is a retail tenant and occupies 60,000 square feet of
   space on the first floor. The lease is for 5 years with one additional 5-year
   renewal option at a discounted rate noted on the breakdown below.
   This tenant is also on a gross lease, and the gross rent is broken down
   next.

Rent Start Date	Rent End Date	Rent
January 1, 2009	December 31, 2009	$4,800,000
January 1, 2010	December 31, 2010	$4,800,000
January 1, 2011	December 31, 2011	$5,000,000
January 1, 2012	December 31, 2012	$5,000,000
January 1, 2013	December 31, 2013	$5,000,000
Renewal Option		
January 1, 2014	December 31, 2014	$4,500,000
January 1, 2015	December 31, 2015	$4,500,000
January 1, 2016	December 31, 2016	$4,700,000
January 1, 2017	December 31, 2017	$4,700,000
January 1, 2018	December 31, 2018	$5,000,000

3. Watkins & Watkins LLP, a law firm, occupies 100,000 square feet of the
   second floor under a 3-year net lease from January 1, 2009, to December
   31, 2011, with one additional 2-year renewal option. The renewal will be
   at market rate at the end of the 3-year lease; therefore, the cost is not
   known at the inception of the lease. The tenant pays $50.00 psf
   throughout the lease term plus its share of operating expenses and real
   estate taxes.

4. ABC & Associates is a regional staffing agency. The firm occupies 100,000
   square feet on the third floor of the building. This net lease is for 5 years
   with 6 months' free rent with no renewal option. A breakdown of the
   lease is:

Rent Start Date	Rent End Date	Rent PSF	Rent
July 1, 2008	December 31, 2008	$ —	$ —
January 1, 2009	December 31, 2009	$45.00	$4,500,000
January 1, 2010	December 31, 2010	$45.00	$4,500,000
January 1, 2011	December 31, 2011	$47.00	$4,700,000
January 1, 2012	December 31, 2012	$47.00	$ 4,700,000
January 1, 2013	June 30, 2013	$50.00	$2,500,000

5. Citizens International Bank occupies 100,000 square feet under fixed
   base lease of $45.00 psf throughout the 3-year lease term from January 1,
   2008 through December 31, 2010 with no renewal option. The operating
   expenses portion of the rent is $15.00 psf. During 2008, the actual

operating expenses were $20.00 psf; thus an additional $5.00 psf would be paid by the tenant.

The breakdown of the rent to be straight-lined is:

Rent Start Date	Rent End Date	Rent PSF	Rent
January 1, 2008	December 31, 2008	$45.00	$4,500,000
January 1, 2009	December 31, 2009	$45.00	$4,500,000
January 1, 2010	December 31, 2010	$47.00	$4,700,000

The five tenants and the applicable lease information are used on the sample rent straight-lining schedule in Exhibit 4.1

Lease Termination

Sometimes prior to a lease expiration the tenant may decide to terminate the lease or default on the lease and therefore be evicted or leave willfully. For GAAP reporting entities, due to the straight-lining of the stream of minimum rental payments and scheduled rent increases when a lease is terminated prior to the lease expiration date, there would be accrued but unpaid rental balance on the balance sheet. This balance is also referred to as deferred rent. Upon the termination of a lease, this deferred rent balance would need to be written off. Unamortized lease costs related to the terminated lease that are not recoverable would have to be written off as well. Some of these unamortized balances would include attorney fees and leasing commissions. Any capital improvements demolished as a result of the tenants vacating the premises would also have to be written off.

MODIFICATION OF AN OPERATING LEASE

Prior to the end of a lease, the lessor and lessee may agree to renew or modify the provisions of the lease. Care must be taken to ensure that the accounting is performed correctly based on the nature of the renewal or modification. Accounting for lease modification is principally governed by FAS 13, paragraph 9, which says:

> If at any time the lessee and lessor agree to change the provisions of the lease, other than by renewing the lease or extending its term, in a manner that would have resulted in a different classification of the lease under the criteria in paragraphs 7 and 8 had the changed terms been in effect at the inception of the lease, the revised agreement shall be considered as a new agreement over its

Exhibit 4.1 Sample Rent Straight-lining Schedule

Suite #	Tenant	Beneficial Occupancy Date	Expiration Date	Net Rentable Area	Rate	Rent Step Date	Rent Step	Period Length	Year	Annual Rent Payment	Straight-line Amount	Deferred Rent	Cumulative Deferred Rent
101	Roxy Clothing	7/1/2009	6/30/2014	40,000	$ —	7/1/2009	$ —	0.5	2009	$ —	$ 1,680,000	$1,680,000	$1,680,000
					$ 80.00	1/1/2010	80.00	1.0	2010	$ 3,200,000	$ 3,360,000	$ 160,000	$1,840,000
					$ 87.50	1/1/2011	87.50	1.0	2011	$ 3,500,000	$ 3,360,000	$ (140,000)	$1,700,000
					$ 95.00	1/1/2012	95.00	1.0	2012	$ 3,800,000	$ 3,360,000	$ (440,000)	$1,260,000
					$102.50	1/1/2013	102.50	1.0	2013	$ 4,100,000	$ 3,360,000	$ (740,000)	$ 520,000
					$110.00	1/1/2014	110.00	0.5	2014	$ 2,200,000	$ 1,680,000	$ (520,000)	$ —
101	*Roxy Clothing*	*7/1/2009*	*6/30/2014*	*40,000*				*5.0*		*$ 16,800,000*	*$ 16,800,000*	*$ —*	*$ —*
102	ABC Grocery Store	1/1/2009	12/31/2018	60,000	$ 80.00	1/1/2009	80.00	1.0	2009	$ 4,800,000	$ 4,800,000	$ —	$ —
					$ 80.00	1/1/2010	80.00	1.0	2010	$ 4,800,000	$ 4,800,000	$ —	$ —
					$ 83.33	1/1/2011	83.33	1.0	2011	$ 5,000,000	$ 4,800,000	$ (200,000)	$ (200,000)
					$ 83.33	1/1/2012	83.33	1.0	2012	$ 5,000,000	$ 4,800,000	$ (200,000)	$ (400,000)
					$ 83.33	1/1/2013	83.33	1.0	2013	$ 5,000,000	$ 4,800,000	$ (200,000)	$ (600,000)
					$ 75.00	1/1/2014	75.00	1.0	2014	$ 4,500,000	$ 4,800,000	$ 300,000	$ (300,000)
					$ 75.00	1/1/2015	75.00	1.0	2015	$ 4,500,000	$ 4,800,000	$ 300,000	$ —
					$ 78.33	1/1/2016	78.33	1.0	2016	$ 4,700,000	$ 4,800,000	$ 100,000	$ 100,000
					$ 78.33	1/1/2017	78.33	1.0	2017	$ 4,700,000	$ 4,800,000	$ 100,000	$ 200,000
					$ 83.33	1/1/2018	83.33	1.0	2018	$ 5,000,000	$ 4,800,000	$ (200,000)	$ —
102	*ABC Grocery Store*	*1/1/2009*	*12/31/2018*	*60,000*				*10.0*		*$ 48,000,000*	*$ 48,000,000*	*$ —*	*$ —*
201	Watkins & Watkins LLP	1/1/2009	12/31/2011	100,000	$ 50.00	1/1/2009	50.00	1.0	2009	$ 5,000,000	$ 5,000,000	$ —	$ —
					$ 50.00	1/1/2010	50.00	1.0	2010	$ 5,000,000	$ 5,000,000	$ —	$ —
					$ 50.00	1/1/2011	50.00	1.0	2011	$ 5,000,000	$ 5,000,000	$ —	$ —

					Price	Date	Factor	Year				
201	**Watkins & Watkins LLP**	**1/1/2009**	**12/31/2011**	**100,000**			**3.0**		**$15,000,000**	**$15,000,000**	**$ —**	**$ —**
301	ABC & Associates	7/1/2008	12/31/2008	100,000	$ —	7/1/2008	0.5	2008	$ —	$ —	$2,090,000	$2,090,000
					$112.50	1/1/2009	1.0	2009	$4,500,000	$2,090,000	$4,180,000	$1,770,000
					$112.50	1/1/2010	1.0	2010	$4,500,000	($320,000)	$4,180,000	$1,450,000
					$117.50	1/1/2011	1.0	2011	$4,700,000	($320,000)	$4,180,000	$930,000
					$117.50	1/1/2012	1.0	2012	$4,700,000	($520,000)	$4,180,000	$410,000
					$125.00	1/1/2013	0.5	2013	$2,500,000	($520,000)	$2,090,000	$ —
										($410,000)		
301	**ABC & Associates**	**7/1/2008**	**12/31/2008**	**100,000**			**5.0**		**$20,900,000**	**$20,900,000**	**$ —**	**$ —**
401	Citizens Int. Bank	1/1/2008	12/31/2010	100,000	$45.00		1.0	2008	$4,500,000	$4,500,000	$ —	$ —
					$45.00		1.0	2009	$4,500,000	$4,500,000	$ —	$ —
					$45.00		1.0	2010	$4,500,000	$4,500,000	$ —	$ —
401	**Citizens Int. Bank**	**1/1/2008**	**12/31/2010**	**100,000**			**3.0**		**$13,500,000**	**$13,500,000**	**$ —**	**$ —**

term, and the criteria in paragraphs 7 and 8 shall be applied for purposes of classifying the new lease. Likewise, except when a guarantee or penalty is rendered inoperative as described in paragraphs 12 and 17(e), any action that extends the lease beyond the expiration of the existing lease term such as the exercise of a lease renewal option other than those already included in the lease term, shall be considered as a new agreement . . . . Changes in estimates (for example, changes in estimates of the economic life or of the residual value of the leased property) or changes in circumstances (for example, default by the lessee), however, shall not give rise to a new classification of a lease for accounting purposes.[1]

The primary purpose here is the discussion of lease modification of an operating lease, not capital, leveraged, or financing leases. For operating leases, any extension or renewal of the terms of the original lease prior to the end of the lease should be accounted for as a new lease. Some of the more common modifications in an operating lease include extension or shortening of the lease term, changes in the minimum lease payment, and changes on the determination of contingent rental income. Even though accounting pronouncements describe that any change to the terms of an operating lease should be accounted for as a new lease, there are industry exceptions. Examples include where a lease is renewed toward the expiration of a lease in the ordinary course of business. As we all know, it is in the best interests of both the lessor and lessee, and it also is common industry practice, for the parties to negotiate and execute a lease renewal before the end of the existing lease. If such renewals occur very close to the expiration, with immaterial impact on original lease balances such as the unamortized lease costs and deferred rents, the straight-lining of the original lease should be allowed to run its course without modification, and the renewal should be accounted for as a new lease starting after the original expiration.

Other than this exception, any extension or renewal of an operating lease should be accounted for as a new lease on the modification date. As mentioned earlier, as a result of the rent straight-lining there may be deferred rent balances on the modification date. Any such deferred rent balance from the original lease on the modification date should be amortized over the remaining life of the original lease plus the new extended lease term. Any unamortized costs, such as attorney's fees and broker's commissions from the original lease, should be amortized over the same period as the deferred rent balance.

---

1. Financial Accounting Standard Board, Financial Accounting Standard No. 13, Accounting for Leases (Norwalk, CT, 1976).

Example

Assume a landlord spent $50,000 and $200,000 on attorney's fees and broker's commissions respectively on a 5-year lease. These costs are being amortized over the lease term. At the end of the third year, the lease was extended for an additional 3 years after the end of the original lease.

The unamortized cost at the end of year 3 and adjusted annual amortization would be determined in this way:

Attorney fees	$50,000	
Broker's commission	$200,000	
Total	$250,000	(a)
Original lease term (years)	5	
Annual amortization	$50,000	
Number of years already amortized	3	
Total amortization at end of year 3	$150,000	(b)
Unamortized balance	$100,000	(a–b)
Remaining years after modification	5	
Modified annual amortization	$20,000	

The deferred rent balances for the same lease would then be accounted for similarly to the deferred cost treatment noted.

SUBLEASE OF OPERATING LEASE

A sublease is an arrangement in which the lessee releases leased premises to another party, generally called a sublessee. In this arrangement, the original lessee of the lease becomes the sublessor.

There are three main types of a sublease:

1. The lessee on the original lease sublets the premises to a third party while still being the obligor under the term of the original lease. Thus there is no modification to the original lease.

2. A new lessee is brought in to replace the original lessee. However, even though the new lessee is primarily responsible and liable in event of default, the original lessee may or may not be secondarily responsible and liable in case of default.

3. The original lease is canceled and a new lease is entered into with a new lessee.

In any of these examples, the new lessee always treats the lease as a new lease, and it is accounted for accordingly. However, the accounting by the original lessor and original lessee varies depending on the type of sublease.

Accounting by the Original Lessor

1. If the lessee sublets the premises to a new lessee without any change to the original lease, then the lessor would not need to change the accounting of the original lease on its books.

2. If a new lessee is brought in to replace the original lessee with the new lessee primarily responsible and liable in event of default, then the lessor should account for it as a termination of the original lease and the start of a new lease with the new third-party lessee.

3. If the original lease with the original lessee is canceled and a new lease is entered with the new lessee, the original lessor should account for it as a termination of the original lease and the start of a new lease.

Accounting by the Original Lessee

1. If the original lessee leases the premises to a third party without any modification to the original lease, the original lessee, as the sublessor under the operating lease, would continue to account for the original lease without any modification and would account for the new lease with the new lessee similarly to the way a lessor would account for an operating lease discussed earlier.

2. If a new lessee is brought in to replace the original lessee as the primary obligee even though the original lessee is still secondarily responsible, the original lessee should account for it as a termination. If applicable, a loss contingency should be recorded.

3. If the original lease is canceled and a new lease is entered with a third party, the original lessee should account for it as a lease termination as well.

5

ACCOUNTING FOR OPERATING PROPERTY EXPENSES

Numerous costs are incurred in the operation of a property. Some of these costs can be recovered from tenants, depending on the lease. Thus, costs are sometimes distinguished as recoverable and nonrecoverable costs. Proper recording of these costs is also very important since not all costs are expensed the year they are incurred. Some costs are deferred and amortized over the useful or beneficial periods.

OPERATING COSTS

Some of the more common types of costs incurred in an operating property are:

1. Property taxes
2. Cleaning services
3. Security
4. Water
5. Electricity
6. Heating, ventilation, and air conditioning (HVAC)
7. Payroll
8. Insurance

   9. Repairs and maintenance

10. Leasing costs

11. Loan closing costs

12. Management fees

13. Sales and use taxes

14. Additional services bill-backs

Property Taxes

Generally property taxes are billed by the city or municipality where the property is located. Property tax is a major source of revenue to local governments and a major expense line on a property's income statement. The amount of taxes paid on a property is assessed by the government taxing agency. The importance of this cost is very evident upon review of a property's financial statement. It is usually one of the largest costs of operating a property. Most taxing authorities give property owners the right to challenge the assessment value used in determining the property taxes. Attorneys and other professionals specialize in helping owners to obtain a fair assessment of their property and thereby reduce their property taxes. Most of these professionals are paid on a contingency basis based on the successful reduction of the taxes. In some cases, their fees can be up to 30 percent of the annual tax reduction. This can be a very profitable profession, especially in cities where property taxes on commercial properties are in the millions a year.

Property tax billing varies between cities. Some cities bill monthly or quarterly while some bill semiannually or annually. However, regardless of how often the property taxes are paid by the owner, the cost should be expensed over the applicable tax period. For some municipalities, property taxes are paid in advance; for others, they are paid in arrears. The bill should be thoroughly reviewed to ensure that the amounts are expensed during the correct period. Assume that a municipality bills property taxes in advance semiannually. In this case, the payment by the property should be recorded as prepaid property taxes when paid and expensed pro rata over the six months.

Example

If on January 1, 2009 the property owner paid $600,000 for property taxes for the period January 1, 2009 through June 30, 2009, the initial and subsequent monthly journal entries would be:

On January 1, 2009:

Prepaid property taxes	$600,000	
Cash		$600,000

(to record property taxes paid for period January 1,
2009 through June 30, 2009)
Monthly starting January 1, 2009:
Property tax expense $100,000
Prepaid property taxes $100,000
(to recognize property tax expense for the month)

At the end of the first month, the prepaid taxes balance would be:

Original prepaid property taxes $600,000
Property taxes expense in January 2009   <u>$100,000</u>
Prepaid taxes balance at January 31, 2009 $500,000

Assume instead of in advance, property taxes for the period of January 1,
2009 through June 30, 2009 are due and paid on June 30, 2009.

In this case the property owner would still have to recognize property
tax expense each month by recording an accrual each month. The required
monthly journal entries would be:

Monthly journal entries starting January 31, 2009:
Property tax expense $100,000
   Accrued property taxes $100,000
(to accrue monthly property taxes due June 30, 2009)

Journal entry on June 30, 2009:
Accrued property taxes $600,000
   Cash $600,000
(to record payment for property taxes for January 1, 2009
through June 30, 2009 due on June 30, 2009)

These entries ensure that the property's financial statement appropriately reflects the property tax expenses every reporting period.

Cleaning

Cleaning involves the cost of cleaning both inside and outside of the property. This service is either provided by the property owner's personnel or
outsourced to third-party cleaning companies. If it is performed by the owner's personnel, this cost would be part of payroll expenses. Cleaning cost is a
period cost and should be expensed during the applicable periods. Therefore, the journal entry to record this type of expense would be:

Cleaning expense $ xx.xx
   Cash or Accounts Payable $ xx.xx

However, in an outsourced cleaning scenario, the parties might agree that the owner would pay in advance every six months. In this case, the amount paid in advance would be a prepaid asset and amortized over the beneficial period. Assume the landlord paid $120,000 for cleaning service for the period January 1, 2009 to June 30, 2009, and this amount was paid on January 1, 2009. The initial and monthly entries would be:

January 1, 2009:

Prepaid cleaning expenses	$120,000	
Cash		$120,000

(to record prepaid cleaning for period January 1, 2009 –June 30, 2009)

Monthly starting January 1, 2009:

Cleaning Expense	$20,000	
Prepaid assets—cleaning		$20,000

(to record monthly clean expense (120,000/ 6 = $20,000)

Security

Security expenses are payments to security companies for providing their security personnel to the property. The services provided by these personnel could include registering guests entering the building, confirming guest visits with the hosting tenant, issuing security passes (IDs) to tenants, surveillance of the exterior and hallways of the building, and a host of other responsibilities.

The fees paid for these services are expensed during the applicable periods similar to the cleaning service discussed earlier. The joined entry recorded for the charge is:

Security services expense	$xx	
Cash or Accounts Payable		$xx

Water, Electricity, HVAC

Water, electricity, and HVAC represent major expense lines in an operating property income statement. The charges for these items are billed by the utility provider to the property. In some cases, where there are submetering arrangements, these charges can be billed directly to tenants. Submetering prevents the allocation of these costs by the landlord using tenants' pro rata shares of the building. Instead, meters are installed for every tenant in the building.

The entries to record these types of charges are:

Water expense	$xx	
Acquired expense		$xx
Electricity expense	$xx	
Acquired expense		$xx
HVAC expense	$xx	
Acquired expense		$xx

Payroll

Payroll includes the compensation cost of all the personnel who perform work for the property. It also includes all employees' employment benefits. Some personnel commonly found at the property include the property managers, engineers, accountants, administrative assistants, and bookkeepers. All compensation to these individuals is recorded as payroll expense.

The entry to record payroll expenses is:

Payroll expense	$xx.xx	
Cash or Accounts Payable		$xx.xx

Insurance

The insurance category represents the cost of purchasing insurance coverage for the property. The amount paid to the insurance company is called the insurance premium. Depending on the insurance company and the arrangement with the property owner, the insurance premiums can be due monthly, quarterly, or annually. Premiums usually are paid in advance. When premiums are paid in advance, they should be recorded as a prepaid expense and amortized over the coverage period.

Assume the property owner paid $30,000 on January 1, 2009 for insurance coverage for the period starting on January 1, 2009 and ending on June 30, 2009. The entry to be recorded on January 1, 2009 when the amount was paid would be:

Prepaid insurance	$30,000	
Cash		$30,000

Therefore, at the end of each month, an entry would need to be recorded to recognize the insurance expense. This entry would be:

Insurance expense	$5,000	
Prepaid insurance		$5,000

At the end of the first month, the balance of prepaid insurance would be ($30,000 – $5,000) $25,000.

Repairs and Maintenance

Repairs and Maintenance are costs spent to keep the property for its intended use. Examples include repair of broken windows and doors, repair of toilets stoppage, replacement of light bulbs, maintenance of the heating system and air conditioner, maintenance of elevators, and so on. Numerous costs fall into this type of expense.

Repairs and Maintenance expenses are period costs and should be expensed as incurred. The entry to record the cost is:

Repairs and Maintenance expenses $xx.xx	
Cash or Accounts Payable	$xx.xx

Leasing Costs

Leasing costs are the costs incurred to lease the premises to tenants. The most common leasing costs are broker's commissions and legal fees. Broker's commissions are paid to brokers for securing a tenant who leases the premises. In a residential lease, the commission is typically paid at lease signing and the payment obligation varies between the landlord and the tenant. In commercial leases, the broker's commission payments are typically spread over the length of the lease and are specified in the commission agreement between the leasing broker and the landlord. The most common commission agreement entitles the broker to a portion of the commission upon a tenant's signing of the lease; the remainder is paid over the term of the lease. Sometimes the landlord and broker may agree that the broker is entitled to an additional commission if the tenant renews at the end of the original lease.

The accounting journal entry to record broker's commission is different from how some of the other costs described above are recorded. The total commission is recorded as a prepaid expense and amortized over the length of the lease.

Example

Assume the broker and landlord agree that the total broker's commission for a 5-year lease with a commencement date of January 1, 2009 and expiration date of December 31, 2013 is $600,000, of which $300,000 is paid upon lease signing with the remaining $300,000 paid on January 1, 2011. Assume the lease was signed on November 15, 2008.

The entry to be recorded upon signing the lease and payment of $300,000 to the broker would be:

Prepaid broker's commission	$600,000	
Accrued broker's commission		$300,000
Cash		$300,000

Thereafter, during the lease period (January 1, 2009–December 31, 2013), the monthly entry to record the amortization of the prepaid broker's commission would be:

Total commission	= $600,000
Number of months	= 60
Monthly amortization	= $10,000

Amortization expense: broker's commission	$10,000	
Accumulated amortization: broker's commission		$10,000

Then at January 1, 2011, when the remainder of the broker's commission is paid, the entry would be:

Accrued broker's commission	$300,000	
Cash		$300,000

Legal fees are the fees paid to an attorney for drafting the tenant lease agreement. In most leases the legal fees are paid upon signing the lease. Regardless of when they are due or paid, the amount should be capitalized and amortized over the term of the lease.

Example

Assume that for the same lease transaction just discussed, the landlord paid $60,000 in legal fees. The entry required upon signing the lease would be:

Prepaid legal fees	$60,000	
Accrued legal fees		$60,000

When the legal fees are paid, the required journal entry would be:

Accrued legal fees	$60,000	
Cash		$60,000

Each month during the lease term, the amount of legal fees to be expensed is calculated as:

Total legal fees	= $60,000
Number of months	= 60
Monthly expense	= $1,000

Amortization expense—legal fees	$1,000	
Prepaid legal fees		$1,000

Loan Closing Costs

In practice, the purchase of real estate in most developed economies is mostly financed with debt. Debt financing involves costs such as application fees, origination fees, administration fees, and syndication costs, among others. These costs are called loan closing costs. These costs should be capitalized and amortized over the life of the loan.

Assume debt was used to finance a real estate asset purchase and the total loan closing costs were $500,000 on a 10-year debt financing. The entry to record the loan closing costs is:

Loan closing costs (assets)	$500,000	
Cash		$500,000

The monthly amortization of this cost during the loan period would be:

Total loan closing costs	= $500,000
Loan period in months	= 120
Monthly amortization	= $4,166.67

The monthly journal entry would be:

Amortization expense—loan closing cost	$4,166.67	
Accumulated amortization—loan closing cost		$4,166.67

Management Fee

In some cases the owner of a real estate entity hires a professional real estate management firm to manage the property. These firms provide the staffing, interface with the tenants, lease vacant space, procure supplies, and collect rents, among other responsibilities.

Management fees are recorded as assets when paid and amortized over the engagement management period unless the amounts are paid periodically over the management period.

Sales and Use Taxes

Sales tax is a state tax on the retail sale of tangible personal property or services. Sale taxes are normally collected by the seller from the purchaser on behalf of the state. The seller in this capacity acts as the custodian for the state in collecting these taxes.

Use tax is a government tax on the use or consumption of tangible personal property or for services where sales tax was not charged by the seller at the time of the transaction. Generally, goods used in a manufacturing capacity are tax exempt because they are part of inventory. Use taxes arise because sometimes, during the purchase, the purchaser has not decided whether the goods would be consumed by the purchaser or used in the production of a final product. If the purchaser ends up using or consuming the goods, the purchaser has to pay use tax to the state.

A purchaser is subject to sales or use tax on tangible personal property if three conditions are met:

1. There is transfer of title or possession.

2. There is transfer of the right to use or control.

3. There is transfer of consideration such as credit, money, or extinguishment of debt.

Note that sales and use taxes are not required on intangible personal property; however, services are subject to sales and use taxes. Care should be taken to differentiate between intangible personal properties and services.

Certain purchasers and products are exempt from sales and use taxes. Examples of exempt purchasers include government agencies, religious organizations and societies, educational organizations, and charitable organizations. Some products exempt from these taxes include donations to nonprofit organizations, publications, research and development, and tangible goods used in the manufacturing, processing, or production of inventory for sale. It is also important to note that different states have different rules on exempt purchasers and products.

Rental income is also exempt from sales or use tax. Landlords' charges for overtime freight elevator service, overtime cleaning, heating, air conditioning services, and electricity are also exempt from sales or use tax because tax rules consider them as incidental to the rental of the premises.

Additional Services Bill-backs

In some cases tenants may require additional services above and beyond the normal level of service agreed to on a lease. These may include requests for HVAC after normal work hours, additional security, or cleaning during certain events. These types of costs are billed back to the requesting tenant and not included as part of operating expenses billed to all tenants.

These additional costs are recorded differently depending on whether the books and records of the property are kept on a GAAP or federal tax basis. On a GAAP basis, the additional billing to the tenant is included as revenue with the corresponding cost recorded as expense. On a federal tax basis, this additional billing is not reported as revenue unless there is a profit earned on this transaction by the property, which would then be reported as revenue.

6

OPERATING EXPENSES RECONCILIATION AND RECOVERIES

As discussed in Chapter 4, certain tenant leases may require that the tenant pay a minimum base rent in addition to its prorated share of operating expenses. This chapter discusses the types of expenses that can be recovered from tenants and the reconciliation process involved.

The typical lease that requires tenants to pay their prorated share of operating expenses normally requires that during the course of the year, tenants pay the landlord an estimated prorated share monthly. At the end of the year, when the actual operating expense can be determined, the landlord performs a reconciliation of operating expenses and refunds or bills tenants for overpayments or underpayments. In some instances, large tenants may require the landlord to pay interest on any overpayment in the estimate after an agreed-on threshold. The interest rate normally is agreed to by the parties and is specified on the lease.

Not all costs incurred by the landlord are recoverable from tenants. What is recoverable or nonrecoverable depends on what the parties agree to. For example, some retail tenants may negotiate that any costs related to the building's elevator should not be included in recoverable operating expense since, if the tenant is on the first floor, it would not have any use for the elevator. However, if the lease is silent on this issue, some landlords may include elevator-related costs in recoverable operating expenses.

MOST COMMON RECOVERABLE OPERATING EXPENSES

Common examples of recoverable operating expenses are:

- Wages and salaries
- Cleaning
- Security
- Electricity
- Water
- Heating, ventilation, and air conditioning (HVAC)
- Repairs and maintenance
- Insurance
- Management fees
- Property taxes

MOST COMMON NONRECOVERABLE OPERATING EXPENSES

Examples of nonrecoverable expenses include:

- Interest on loans
- Certain depreciation and amortization expenses
- Penalties, fines, and late charges
- Capital improvements
- Office supplies
- Executive compensation
- Contributions and donations
- Employee entertainment and parties
- Cost of furnishing management company office located at the property
- Income taxes
- Leasing costs
- Financing costs

- Legal fees

- Advertising and promotional costs

- Costs of any judgments, settlements, or arbitrations

- Professional dues of employees

These nonrecoverable costs are deemed landlord's expenses and therefore not the responsibility of the tenants. The list is not all inclusive. Tenants can negotiate many other costs to be omitted from recoverable operating expenses.

CALCULATING TENANT PRO-RATA SHARE OF EXPENSES

Usually, prior to the beginning of the year, the landlord puts together a budget for the following year that shows the estimated operating expenses and property taxes recoveries from each tenant. Each tenant would then pay its pro-rated share on a monthly basis throughout the year. At the end of the year, the landlord performs a reconciliation to determine if the tenant overpaid or underpaid during the course of the year. In some cases a midyear reconciliation can be performed to determine if the monthly payment should be adjusted.

Assume the landlord's estimate recoverable operating expense for the following year is as indicated:

Estimated Operating Expenses Recoveries	
Wages & salaries	$390,000
Cleaning	$100,000
Security	$95,000
Electricity	$100,000
Water	$50,000
HVAC	$50,000
Repairs	$45,000
Insurance	$100,000
Management fees	$120,000
Property taxes	$150,000
Total Recoverable Operating Expenses	$1,200,000

Let us assume now that at the end of that year, the actual recoverable operating expenses were determined to be:

Actual Operating Expenses Recoveries

Wages & salaries	$435,000
Cleaning	$115,000
Security	$103,000
Electricity	$120,000
Water	$75,000
HVAC	$46,000
Repairs	$81,000
Insurance	$130,000
Management fees	$120,000
Property taxes	$175,000
Total Recoverable Operating Expenses	$1,400,000

In this example, the total estimated recoverable operating expenses were $1,200,000; however, the actual amount came in at $1,400,000. This additional recovery would then be billed to the tenants based on their pro-rata share of operating expenses.

Assume one of the tenants in the building, AB Mgt. LLC, occupies 20,000 square feet of space and has operating expenses at a pro-rata share of 5.25%. This tenant must have paid the listed amount monthly to the landlord for estimated operating expenses prior to the reconciliation at the end of the year:

Total Estimated Operating Expenses	$1,200,000
AB Mgt. LLC pro-rata share	5.25%
AB Mgt. LLC Estimated Annual Share	$63,000
AB Mgt. Estimated Monthly Share	$5,250

Therefore, for AB Mgt., as for other tenants, the additional operating expenses recoveries to be paid to landlord after the reconciliation would be:

Actual Recoverable Operating Expenses	$1,400,000
Estimated Recoverable Operating Expenses	$1,200,000
Additional Recoverable Operating Expenses	$200,000
AB Mgt. pro-rata share	5.25%
AB Mgt. Additional Recoverable Operating Expenses	$10,500

The calculation would be done for each of the tenants in the building. As discussed earlier, the actual recoverable operating expenses may vary between tenants since some tenants may negotiate with the landlord not to include certain costs. So, for some tenants the actual recoverable operating expenses could be more or less than the $1,400,000 used in the AB Mgt. calculation.

The recovery of capital improvement is treated differently from the other costs. Capital improvements in most cases have beneficial or useful life of more than one year. So, these types of costs are not recovered from tenants fully during the year they are incurred; rather, they are recovered over their beneficial period through depreciation of the costs. An example of capital improvement is the modernization of a building's elevator. The lease generally indicates the number of years these types of costs can be recovered from tenants.

An example may help clarify this further. Assume a landlord spends a total of $400,000 in modernizing six elevators during 2009. The modernization has a useful life of 20 years. The annual recovery for this cost would be:

Total cost of the Capital improvement	$400,000
Capital improvement useful life (in years)	20
Annual recovery	$20,000

This $20,000 would be included as part of actual recoverable operating expenses annually for 20 years instead of $400,000 for 1 year.

7

LEASE INCENTIVES AND TENANT IMPROVEMENTS

LEASE INCENTIVES

Lease incentives are payments made by a lessor to or on behalf of a lessee to entice the lessee to sign a lease. Lease incentives may include up-front cash payments to the lessee, payment of costs on behalf of the lessee (such as moving expenses), termination fees to lessee's prior landlord, or lessor's assumption of lessee's lease obligation under a different lease with another landlord.

Lease incentives are sometimes called tenant inducements and should be accounted for as reductions of rental expenses by the lessee and as reductions of rental revenue by the lessor on a straight-line basis over the term of the lease.

In a lease incentive arrangement in which the lessor agrees to assume the lessee's prior lease with a prior landlord, any estimated loss from the assumption of that lease by the lessor would need to be recognized over the term of the new lease by the lessor. Financial Accounting Standards Board, Technical Bulletin No. 88-1, *Issues Relating to Accounting for Leases (Norwalk CT: 1988),* allows the lessor and the lessee to independently estimate any loss as a result of the lessor's assumption of the lease; thus, both parties can have different measurements and record different estimated losses.

According to paragraph 8:

the lessee's estimate of the incentive could be based on a comparison of the new lease with the market rental rate available for similar lease property or the market rental rate from the same lessor without the lease assumption, and the lessor should estimate any loss based on the total remaining costs reduced by the expected benefits from the sublease or use of the assumed leased property.

In addition, any future changes in the estimated loss, such as due to changes in the leasing assumptions, should be accounted as a change in estimates. In accordance with Financial Accounting Standards Board FAS 154, *Accounting Changes and Error Corrections*, and APB Opinion No. 20, Accounting for Changes, it should be recognized during the period in which the change occurred.

Note, however, that the guidance does not change the immediate recognition by the lessee of items such as moving expenses, losses on subleases, and write-offs of abandoned improvements at the old premises.

Example

To illustrate the accounting for a loss on a lessor assumption of the lessee's lease with a third party, let us assume that the lessee signs a 10-year lease with the lessor and the lessor agreed to assume the lessee's lease with a third party that has 3 years remaining. Also assume these other salient terms of the deal:

1. Annual lease payment on the old lease assumed by lessor is $120,000.

2. Annual lease payment by the lessee on the new lease is $250,000.

3. Lessor's estimated annual sublease revenue on the old premises is $110,000.

4. Lessor's estimated total loss from assuming lease is $60,000.

5. Lessee's estimate of the incentive is $50,000.

The proper journal entries to be recorded by the lessor and the lessee would be:

LESSOR JOURNAL ENTRIES

At lease inception:

Lease incentive	$60,000	
Sublease liability		$60,000

(To record the incentive and liability related to loss on assumption of lease)

Annual journal entries in years 1–3:

Sublease liability (60,000/3yr)	$20,000	
Sublease expense	$100,000	
Cash		$120,000

(To record annual sublease payment and amortized sublease liability)

Annual journal entries in years 1–10:

Cash	$250,000	
Rental revenue		$244,000
Lease incentive (60,000/10yrs)		$6,000

(To record revenue on the new lease and amortized lease incentive)

LESSEE JOURNAL ENTRIES

At lease inception:

Loss on lease assumed by new lessor	$50,000	
Incentive from Lessor		$50,000

(To recognize loss on sublease and the related incentive)

Annual journal entries in years 1–10:

Incentives from Lessor ($50,000/10)	$5,000	
Rental Expense	245,000	
Cash		$250,000

(To record annual rental expense and amortization of incentive from lessor)

As you can see, the entries to be recorded by both parties are quite different.

TENANT IMPROVEMENTS

Tenant improvements are capital expenditures made by the landlord to prepare the space for lease. Such improvements are capital assets of the landlord. These improvements are components of the property and therefore should be capitalized and depreciated over their useful life consistent with the accounting for property, plant, and equipment. For tax basis reporting entities, the improvements are depreciated over 39 years on a straight-line basis; however, if any of the investors in the entity are tax-exempt entities, the depreciation would be over 40 years.

TENANT IMPROVEMENT JOURNAL ENTRIES

The journal entry to record expenditures for tenant improvements of $100,000 with a 10-year useful life for a generally accepted accounting principles (GAAP) basis entry would be:

Tenant improvement	$100,000	
Accounts Payable or Cash		$100,000

The recurring annual journal entry to record depreciation of the improvement is:

Depreciation ($100,000/10)	$10,000	
Accumulated depreciation		$10,000

If at any time it was determined that the useful life of this improvement is different from what was anticipated, the annual depreciation should be adjusted going forward in accordance with the accounting for change in estimates. One reason that the useful life of a tenant improvement changes could be that the premises where the improvements were made was subsequently leased to a tenant for an eight-year term, and it is expected that the improvements would no longer be useful at the end of that time. In this case, the depreciable life of these tenant improvements would be through the end of the lease.

Depreciation of tenant improvements should commence as soon as the improvements are substantially complete and the premises are ready for their intended use. If a lease commences while a landlord is still completing tenant improvements, revenue recognition should not start until the tenant improvements are complete, regardless of whether a tenant started paying rent or not. In addition, there could be lease arrangements in which payments made by tenants are appropriately classified as tenant improvements and the landlord paid only a portion of the total cost of the improvements. In a situation like this, the landlord will still record the asset and the usual periodic depreciation; the portion paid by the tenant should still be recorded as asset by the landlord but with a corresponding credit to a deferred liability. The assets should be depreciated over the shorter of the useful life or the lease term; the deferred liability should be amortized to rental revenue on a straight-line basis over the term of the related lease.

FURTHER COMPARISON OF LEASE INCENTIVES AND TENANT IMPROVEMENTS

In recent times there has been considerable confusion regarding what constitutes a lease incentive or tenant improvement. Sometimes it may not be clear whether funds provided by the landlord in connection with a lease represent lease incentives or tenant improvements. Some cases are not clear cut and may require significant judgment and consideration of several factors. Determining whether funds provided by a landlord is a tenant improvement or incentive should be based on the substance and contractual rights of the lessor and lessee. Deloitte & Touche have indicated that factors to consider in determining whether a funding is a tenant improvement or incentive include but are not limited to these seven points:

1. Whether the tenant is obligated by the terms of the lease agreement to construct or install specifically identified assets (i.e., the leasehold improvements) as a condition of the lease.

2. Whether the failure by the tenant to make specified improvements is an event of default under which the landlord can require the lessee to make those improvements or otherwise enforce the landlord's rights to those assets (or a monetary equivalent).

3. Whether the tenant is permitted to alter or remove the leasehold improvements without the consent of the landlord and/or without compensating the landlord for any lost utility or diminution in fair value.

4. Whether the tenant is required to provide the landlord with evidence supporting the cost of tenant improvements prior to the landlord paying the tenant for the tenant improvements.

5. Whether the landlord is obligated to fund cost overruns for the construction of leasehold improvements.

6. Whether the leasehold improvements are unique to the tenant or could reasonably be used by the lessor to lease to other parties.

7. Whether the economic life of the leasehold improvements is such that it is anticipated that a significant residual value of the assets will accrue to the benefit of the landlord at the end of the lease term.[1]

These factors show how complicated some leases can be in determining whether funds provided by a landlord is a lease incentive or tenant improvement.

DIFFERENCES IN CASH FLOW STATEMENT PRESENTATION

After it has been determined whether a funding is a lease incentive or a tenant improvement, the next question should be how this cost should be presented on the cash flow statement. As mentioned earlier, tenant improvements are capital assets and therefore should be presented on the investing activities section of the landlord's cash flow statement. Lease incentives, however, are operating activities and should be presented as such.

DEMOLITION OF BUILDING IMPROVEMENT

Most often when a tenant leaves and the space is leased to a new tenant, the landlord demolishes some improvements related to the space to get it

---

1. Deloitte & Touche, "*Lessor Accounting Issues: Follow Up to Heads Up,*" 12, no. 1 (March 2005).

ready for the new tenant. The question is how the costs of demolition and the removed improvement should be accounted. Internal Revenue Code 168(i)(8)(B) requires that the unrecovered basis of improvements that are demolished should be written off. If a portion of the improvements from the old tenant is to be used by the new tenant, the remaining portion should continue to be depreciated.

8

BUDGETING FOR OPERATING PROPERTIES

WHAT IS A BUDGET?

A budget is a formal business plan set by an organization for future business activities on which actual future activities would be evaluated. It can also be described as a management tool used to communicate management's goals and objectives for a given future period. For an operating property, a budget helps management understand the future outlook of the property, including the revenue streams and expenditures. A well-prepared budget is an important tool used by management in cash flow planning and asset valuation. A budget also communicates management's strategy and sets the tone for both short-term and long-term expectations.

COMPONENTS OF A BUDGET

Normally there are various sections of an operating property budget. However, the level of detail depends on the organization's structure, goals, and objectives. The most common components of a budget are:

1. Executive Summary

    a. Brief description of the entity or assets or both

    b. Discussion of key goals and objectives

    c. Organizational chart

    d. Brief market overview and economic conditions

2. Presentation of the detail budget, commonly made up of:

   a. Revenues

      i. Office rents

      ii. Retail rents

      iii. Residential rents

      iv. Operating expenses recovery

      v. Storage rents

      vi. Antenna rents

      vii. Parking rents

      viii. Interest income

      ix. Investment income

   b. Recoverable operating expenses

      i. Wages and salaries

      ii. Property taxes

      iii. Electricity

      iv. Heating, ventilation, and air conditioning (HVAC)

      v. Cleaning

      vi. Water

      vii. Insurance

      viii. Security

      ix. Management fees

      x. Repairs and maintenance

   c. Nonrecoverable operating expenses

      i. Marketing expenses

      ii. Public relations

      iii. Fines and penalties

      iv. Income taxes

      v. Audit fees

      vi. Ownership legal fees

d. Capital expenditures

    i. Capital improvements

    ii. Leasing commissions

    iii. Lease incentives

    iv. Tenants improvements

    v. Leasing costs

e. Debt servicing

    i. Debt serving costs

    ii. Financing costs

f. Ownership contributions and distributions

    i. Distributions

    ii. Contributions

During the budgeting process, each of the budget categories is broken out to the general ledger account level, and the budgeted amounts for the given year are determined. Determining the most probable amount for each of the account line items requires detailed knowledge of the property; thus, budgeting requires the input of all individuals involved in the operation of the property. Some of the individuals whose inputs are very important in developing an accurate and meaningful budget in an organization include at least:

Property manager

Assistant property managers

Property accountants

Leasing personnel

Property engineers

Asset manager

Now let us discuss some of the budget lines a little further.

Revenues

In budgeting revenue, the preparer would need to be familiar with tenant leases to ensure that all amounts due from the tenants are included. The person in charge of leasing would also need to provide information on leasing assumptions for expected future leases for the period covered by the budget. The operating expense recoveries to be included would then be determined based on the budgeted operating expenses.

Operating Expenses

Detailed knowledge of the building's operations is required to determine operating expenses. This section cannot be estimated accurately without the input of the personnel who run the property, such as the property manager, assistant property manager, and property engineers, among others. The budgeting of operating expenses involves good knowledge of vendor contracts, the condition of the building machinery and equipments, and good understanding of the utilities market and other major expense line items.

Capital Expenditures

Capital expenditures are improvements related to the building and its permanent structures. For budgeting purposes, this section of the budget should also include lease incentives, tenant improvements, leasing commissions, and leasing legal fees. These costs are ownership costs and therefore not recoverable from tenants. However, some tenant leases may allow the landlord to recover the cost of the improvement over time if the improvement helps reduce future operating expenses. An example would be the replacement of an old chiller system with a new cost-effective system.

Debt Servicing

Debt servicing represents the owner's periodic payments to the lender on a loan. The lender could be a bank, financing company, insurance company, or investment firm. Some debt service could be structured as interest-only or principal-plus-interest payments. Also, some financing could be fixed interest payments while some could be variable interest. A thorough understanding of the loan agreement is necessary to ensure that correct amounts are budgeted. For example, a variable interest financing arrangement requires deeper knowledge of movements in interest rates in order to forecast rates in future periods. In cases where interest rates are very volatile, prior years' rates might not be the best guide.

Ownership Distributions and Contributions

Distributions represent payments of excess cash from the entity to the owner(s). This could be as a return on or of investment, depending on the nature and profitability of the entity. Contributions represent the entity owners' funding for shortfalls to the entity. The shortfalls could be as a result of unusual or expected major capital expenditures, such as capital improvements, payment of lease incentives, and tenant improvements or leasing costs.

It is important to note that the categories listed are not all inclusive; a robust budget may require many other categories. In most cases, budgets are quite extensive—up to tens of pages, depending on the nature and complexity of the operation or entity. In some cases, the leasing assumptions alone could be tens of pages, as could the market overview section, which might get into the market's demand and supply.

9

VARIANCE ANALYSIS

In Chapter 8 we described the budget as a management tool that helps management set the direction of the business and also helps communicate management's strategic goal. A variance analysis is the periodic review of actual business results and comparison of them to management's approved budget. This analysis shows the degree of discrepancy between budgets and actual results with explanations of reasons for the discrepancies. A good variance analysis should be thoroughly detailed to help management and other decision makers understand why actual numbers are different from budgets. A variance analysis can be a very powerful management tool because it helps management adjust expectations and also helps to indicate probable issues with the operation of a particular asset or entity. It is good practice to perform variance analysis at least quarterly so that management can be alerted to potential issues in a timely manner.

A well-prepared variance analysis breaks down the numbers such that meaningful budget categories can be compared to the actual results. The level of detail will vary depending on management's needs. Even though it is advisable for the operating team to have a detailed variance analysis, the report presented to top management may only highlight the major variances. A well-performed analysis should present side by side the budgeted and actual results for a given period with explanations for significant variances. Management normally sets variance threshold(s) to determine the degree of variance that would require explanation. If the variances between budgeted amounts and actual results are greater than the threshold, reasons for the variance would have to be explained. Setting thresholds ensures that time is spent on items with significant discrepancies; it is impossible for all actual numbers to tie exactly to budgeted amounts.

SAMPLE OPERATING PROPERTY VARIANCE ANALYSIS

A sample operating property variance analysis is provided in Exhibit 9.1

Exhibit 9.1 Variance Analysis, Six Months Ended June 30, 2009

Account	Year to Date Actual vs. Year to Date Budget					Year Ending Projected vs. Year Ending Budgeted				
	Year to Date Actual	Year to Date Budget	Variance ($)	Variance (%)	Explanation—for variances over $25,000 and 10%	Year Ending Projected	Year Ending Budgeted	Variance ($)	Variance (%)	Explanation—for variances over $25,000 and 10%
REVENUES:										
Base Rent	6,002,500	6,000,000	2,500	0%	No explanation needed.	12,000,000	12,000,000	—	0%	No explanation needed.
Parking Revenue	220,321	250,000	(29,679)	-12%	Parking revenues were down due to road construction down the block that prevented normal flow of traffic and potential daily parking customers. We expect parking revenues to go back to normal level during Q4 2009 when road construction is complete.	450,000	500,000	(50,000)	-10%	Parking revenues were down due to road construction down the block that prevented normal flow of traffic and potential daily parking customers. We expect parking revenues to go back to normal level during Q4 2009 when road construction is complete.
Antenna Revenue	91,666	75,000	16,666	22%	No explanation needed.	216,667	150,000	66,667	44%	WTC Communication signed a 5 yr lease to install 2 antennas. The rental for the 2 antennas is $100,000 annually. The lease commenced on May 1, 2009. The income from this lease for 2009 is $66,667.
Investment Income	12,352	25,000	(12,648)	-51%	No explanation needed.	20,000	50,000	(30,000)	-60%	The decrease in investment income is due to lower than expected interest income on our bank accounts. Due to the state of the U.S. economy the Federal Reserve has been cutting interest rates.
Recoveries										
Operating Expenses Recoveries	1,352,035	1,250,000	102,035	8%	No explanation needed.	2,700,000	2,500,000	200,000	8%	The increase in year ending projected operating expenses recoveries is due to increase in operating expenses which are recoverable from tenants. Most increases are on salaries and utilities. Wages & salaries went up by about $110,000 due to hiring of a new assistant manager, which we initially anticipated to take place in 2010. Utilities are expected to be up about $110,000 due to higher electricity rate than was anticipated.
Property Tax Recoveries	400,000	400,000	—	0%	No explanation needed.	800,000	800,000	—	0%	No explanation needed.
TOTAL REVENUE	8,078,874	8,000,000	78,874			16,186,667	16,000,000	186,667		
OPERATING EXPENSES:										
Recoverables										
Wages and Salaries	635,032	600,000	(35,032)	-6%	No explanation needed.	1,310,000	1,200,000	(110,000)	-9%	No explanation needed.
Cleaning	141,450	150,000	8,550	6%	No explanation needed.	297,000	300,000	3,000	1%	No explanation needed.
Securities	131,000	125,000	(6,000)	-5%	No explanation needed.	256,000	250,000	(6,000)	-2%	No explanation needed.

	Actual	Budget	Variance	%	Explanation	Actual	Budget	Variance	%	Explanation
Utilities	215,938	150,000	(65,238)	-43%	The increase is due to higher electricity rate from our electricity supplier. This higher rate is expected to continue at least throughout the year.	410,000	300,000	(110,000)	-37%	Utilities are expected to be up about $110,000 in 2009 due to higher electricity rate than was anticipated.
Repairs and Maintenance	73,111	75,000	1,889	3%	No explanation needed.	150,000	150,000	—	0%	No explanation needed.
Insurance	30,250	25,000	(5,250)	-21%	No explanation needed.	61,000	50,000	(11,000)	-22%	No explanation needed.
Management Fees	161,577	160,000	(1,577)	-1%	No explanation needed.	323,733	320,000	(3,733)	-1%	No explanation needed.
Property Taxes	400,000	400,000	—	0%	No explanation needed.	800,000	800,000	—	0%	No explanation needed.
Other Recoverable Expenses	26,000	17,500	(8,500)	-49%	No explanation needed.	41,000	35,000	(6,000)	-17%	No explanation needed.
Total Recoverable Expenses	1,813,658	1,702,500	(111,158)			3,648,733	3,405,000	(243,733)		
Nonrecoverables										
Marketing Expenses	23,532	25,000	1,468	6%	No explanation needed.	23,532	25,000	1,468	6%	No explanation needed.
Bad Debt Expenses	5,000	6,000	1,000	17%	No explanation needed.	5,000	12,000	7,000	58%	No explanation needed.
Fines and Penalties	—	2,500	2,500	100%	No explanation needed.	—	5,000	5,000	100%	No explanation needed.
Total Nonrecoverable Expenses	28,532	33,500	4,968			28,532	42,000	13,468		
TOTAL OPERATING EXPENSES	1,842,190	1,736,000	(106,190)			3,677,265	3,447,000	(230,265)		
PROPERTY OPERATING INCOME	6,236,684	6,264,000	(27,316)			12,509,402	12,553,000	(43,598)		
Interest Expense	2,500,000	2,500,000	—			5,000,000	5,000,000	—		
NET OPERATING INCOME (NOI)	3,736,684	3,764,000	(27,316)	0%	No explanation needed.	7,509,402	7,553,000	(43,598)	0%	No explanation needed.
CAPITAL EXPENDITURES:										
Building Improvements	205,450	120,000	(85,450)	-71%	The remodelling of the entrance lobby and elevator replacement cost significantly more than anticipated. The entrance lobby was under budget by $55,000 due to subsequent changes in the design. The elevator replacement ended up costing $40,000 more than the preliminary quotes obtained from the contractors due to additional elevator parts we had thought could be reused but were later determined to be damaged.	205,450	120,000	(85,450)	-71%	The remodelling of the entrance lobby and elevator replacement cost significantly more than anticipated. The entrance lobby was under budget by $55,000 due to subsequent changes in the design. The elevator replacement ended up costing $40,000 more than the preliminary quotes obtained from the contractors due to additional elevator parts we had thought could be reused but were later determined to be damaged.
Lease incentives	150,000	180,000	30,000	17%	The lease incentive negotiated with the lease of the third-floor space to Millman & Judge was $30,000 less than we budgeted.	180,000	200,000	20,000	10%	No explanation needed.
Leasing Commissions	43,568	45,000	1,432	3%	No explanation needed.	60,000	60,000	—	0%	No explanation needed.
Leasing Legal Fees	20,000	20,000	—	0%	No explanation needed.	30,000	30,000	—	0%	No explanation needed.
Other Capital Expenditures	15,000	20,000	5,000	25%	No explanation needed.	15,000	25,000	10,000	40%	No explanation needed.
TOTAL CAPITAL EXPENDITURES	434,018	385,000	(49,018)			490,450	435,000	(55,450)		
Debt Principle Payments	1,200,000	1,200,000	—			2,400,000	2,400,000	—		
CASH FLOWS BEFORE ADJUSTMENTS	2,102,666	2,179,000	(76,334)	0%	No explanation needed.	4,618,952	4,718,000	(99,048)	0%	No explanation needed.

SALIENT POINTS ON A VARIANCE ANALYSIS

Some of the most salient points to note on the variance analysis in Exhibit 9.1 are presented next.

- A reasonable variance threshold should be established based on both the actual dollar variance and the percentage variance. This is because a significant percentage change might not be material in terms of the dollar value.

- Management can set different thresholds for different types of accounts for variance explanation. For example, one threshold might be used for revenue items and another threshold used for expenses or capital improvement amounts.

- The variance explanations should detail the reasons for the variance and, where possible, quantify the different components that resulted in the overall variance for a particular line item.

- Each line on a variance analysis file that does not require any explanation because it is below the threshold should be indicated to ensure that particular line was not mistakenly omitted.

- Favorable outcomes should be indicated as positive variances; unfavorable outcomes should be indicated as negative variances.

- Periodic variance analysis performed prior to year-end should at least include year-to-date actual and budgeted amounts to help the reader better understand the condition of the entity. Some variance analysis provides end-of-year projected amounts.

These key points help to ensure that a variance analysis provides management and decision makers with good insight into the operation of an entity and help to prevent year-end surprises about an asset's or an entity's performance.

10

MARKET RESEARCH AND ANALYSIS

MARKET RESEARCH DEFINED

In the field of real estate, market research is the study of the attributes of a specific geographic area for the primary purpose of making a real estate investment decision. Market research is fundamental for a successful real estate investment decision. It provides a valuable insight into the market's trend and future outlook.

MARKET ANALYSIS DEFINED

Market analysis is the examination of market data obtained from market research to help make real estate investment decisions. In a market analysis, data such as the supply and demand for a specific type of real estate are analyzed and used in the determination of value for a particular piece of real estate. These data also can help in the determination of a real estate parcel's highest and best use. According to Geltner, Miller, Clayton, and Eichholtz:

> Market analysis is typically designed to assist in such decisions as:
>
> - Where to locate a branch office
> - What size or type of building to develop on a specific site
> - What type of tenants to look for in marketing a particular building
> - What the rent and expiration terms should be on a given lease

- When to begin construction on a development project

- How many units to build this year

- Which cities and property types to invest in so as to allocate capital where rents are more likely to grow

- Where to locate new retail outlets and/or which should be closed.[1]

It is important to note that a real estate market research analysis can be undertaken from the perspective of a specific real estate site or multiple sites, or from the perspective of a specific geographic area. Therefore, it is important for the report to clearly indicate its purpose.

MARKET RESEARCH: PRACTICAL PROCESS

A complete market research and analysis should be able to give the user a good sense of the subject market or subject property and help the user make decisions. The provider of a market research report should first understand the objective and intended purpose of the report.

There are two main scenarios in which market research is utilized:

1. Investor(s) or developer (s) searching for site for a known project type

2. Investor(s) or developer(s) with a known site evaluating the highest and best use of a site

In both scenarios, good market research will be needed to help make this important decision. Market research is usually documented in the form of a report that gives users all the important information about the market and/or property. Also, in most cases the market research is provided as a section in a real estate appraisal. In this case it becomes one of the tools that the appraiser uses in determining an estimate of value for the property.

In a market research and analysis, a good deal of time is spent in understanding the geographic area, including the market's demand and supply mechanism for that particular real estate type (e.g., residential apartment, condominium, cooperative housing, office space, hotel, shopping mall, etc.). The report should look into the factors that affect that particular market and how shifts in these factors would affect future supply and demand.

---

1. David M. Geltner, Norman G. Miller, Jim Clayton, and Piet Eichholtz, *Commercial Real Estate Analysis & Investment* (Mason, OH: Thomson South-Western, 2007), p. 103.

Some of the factors usually discussed in the report include:

- Population and demographic trends
- Income
- Education level
- Transportation
- Availability of public facilities: amenities, healthcare, recreational facilities
- Crime rate and trends
- Government regulations and restrictions
- Competing projects, both current and ongoing
- Availability of sites and existing properties
- Homeownership culture
- Employment

The next sections discuss some of these salient facts and how they could impact an investor's decision on whether to invest in a particular market.

Population and Demographic Trends

No market research is complete without a thorough understanding of the population and demographic trends of the market. This would include understanding the historical and projected future population growth and also the proportion of the population in different age groups. Whether 20 or 60 percent of a population is made up of people ages 20 to 30 years or 60 to 70 years is very important in understanding the market and its real estate needs. It also helps investors in decision making. Some of the main sources of U.S. population information include the U.S. census data (www. census.gov) and local government information. Some private organizations also provide these data for a fee. Available information on population usually includes ethnic composition of the population and population growth trends. Other information includes the culture and language predominant in the area and average household size, among others.

Income

One source of income data for a particular geographical area is the U.S. census. This information is very important, especially in a potential residential property investment. Depending on the type of property, the investor needs to make sure it is positioned to attract the most profitable group. Certain projects are more profitable for occupancy by certain income groups, and profitability affects the viability of the project. The income growth for an area needs to be looked at also; some areas could be experiencing a negative growth trend due to residents leaving the area for better locations. Income level also indicates the purchasing power of the neighborhood. Obviously, the higher the disposable income, the more people tend to spend. Some sources of information on buying power and consumer spending include the U.S. Department of Labor and state Departments of Labor and employment commissions websites.

Education Level

Companies tend to locate where they can find qualified employees. Therefore, market research should discuss the educational composition of the subject neighborhood. Normally the higher the education level, the higher the income and thus disposable income. Knowledge of the educational composition of an area being considered for investment is very important and cannot be overstated. The types of amenities to include in a property tend to be of higher quality when dealing with people of higher education and thus income, so knowledge of this information would help in the detailed planning of any type of investment targeted toward this group.

Transportation

Of all the factors to consider in a study of a market, including determining where to build or invest, one of the most important things to consider is transportation. Transportation changes neighborhoods. Access to major means of transportation brings people from all corners to the neighborhood. The impact of transportation is very evident in a commercial business district (CBD). Even within a CBD, the proximity of a particular property to a major transportation hub is reflected in the rent the property can command in relation to similar properties in the same CBD. This characteristic of transportation is common in most major cities in the world.

Availability of Public Facilities

Similar to transportation, the availability of public facilities, such as hospitals, healthcare centers, parks, and recreational facilities, contributes tremendously to a neighborhood. These facilities bring people to the neighborhood and drive economic growth there. The availability of public facilities means that investors and developers do not need to spend their own funds to provide such facilities, which help in the economic growth of an area. The availability of these facilities through the government also means that the government helps drive economic growth; a city's planning initiative should be looked at in making real estate investment decisions. In addition, facilities such as hospitals and health centers employ a large number of people, from doctors, to healthcare administrators, to day laborers; thus, the demand for housing and support services increases significantly in such areas.

Crime Rate

Nothing kills a neighborhood more than crime. Safety is one of the most important things people consider when determining where to live or work. Numerous surveys have shown the inverse relationship between crime rates and house prices. Nobody wants to put his or her life in harm's way. Cities are more prosperous and vibrant when citizens feel safe in going about their business. Government can make a difference in encouraging economic growth by reducing crime. The safer an area, the more likely companies will move in and the more likely companies will find potential employees. Employees would tend to spend time and money in safe areas, which all leads to more economic growth and better social life.

Government Regulations and Restrictions

The government, usually in the form of city or municipal government, controls land use through zoning and permits. Zoning determines the type, height, and set-back of buildings in different parts of the community. Through zoning, the government determines whether certain areas should be commercial, residential, industrial, or mixed use. It is important to note that there are cities in the United States without zoning restrictions; the best known is Houston, Texas. The government also restricts what gets built through the issuance of building permits. The government's goal is not just to restrict development but to manage or direct what gets built. The government also uses its power to promote certain useful public policy in communities, especially in ensuring that the middle class are not driven out of certain neighborhoods due to the rising cost of real estate. Governments do this through various programs, such as requiring that new residential projects have a certain percentage of units dedicated to low-income earners, giving property tax abatements for properties with a certain percentage of units allocated to lower-income earners, and guaranteeing some loans on projects that support the government's initiative. Government uses many ways to encourage or restrict projects.

Competing Projects

Market research should give the user information on competition in that particular market. Competition includes existing properties, ongoing projects, approved projects not started, and planned projects not yet submitted for approval. Existing properties are the stocks of similar properties currently in use in that market. Market research helps investors understand the market better, including knowing who the major players in the market are. It also helps in coming up with products with competitive advantage. Knowledge of ongoing projects and others not yet begun is even more important because of the demand-and-supply mechanism. Oversupply of a particular type of property in the market leads to reduction in rents as potential tenants have more choices. Information on ongoing projects and on those approved but not begun can be obtained from the department of buildings in the area under consideration. Information on conceived projects not yet submitted for approval can be the most difficult to obtain, but local newspapers are good sources of data on major projects.

Availability of Sites end Existing Properties

Information on available vacant lots can help give a developer an idea of the market and insight on what is available and the possible sites in which to invest. It also helps estimate future supply in that market. For investments in existing property, investors use information on most recent transactions and currently available properties for sale to determine if a particular market meets their investment criteria. Some important information that can be obtained on these transactions includes the rent per square foot, purchase and sales price per square foot, and cost of operation, among others. Information on completed transactions can be obtained from the municipality department of finance or similar agencies, depending on the state. This information can also be obtained from private organizations that keep track of real estate transactions, such as the Costar website. Information on available sites and properties can also be obtained from major real estate brokerage firms in that market.

Homeownership Culture

An understanding of homeownership is very important in real estate, especially in residential real estate investment. Investors need to understand the homeownership culture and the willingness of the residents to own their own homes or rent apartments in and around the subject market.

Investors have to consider how homeownership would affect the planned investment. The study should consider not just current ownership composition but the trend, and then look at where things are going while bearing in mind that the past does not always predict the future absolutely.

Employment

Employment opportunities bring people to a particular geographic area. This is more evident in CBDs, where companies are usually concentrated and therefore bring in more people and activities. The unemployment rate of the subject market should be well understood, including knowledge of the major industries in the market. Knowledge of the major local industries helps investors better understand the employment situation including its drivers and also helps them better understand how that market can be impacted by economic slowdowns in certain industries.

The factors presented in this chapter are some, but not all, of the ones that should be addressed by a market research report and should be well understood by all real estate investors and developers. They are the key salient factors that investors should expect in a market research report; they can make a different between success and failure.

Exhibit 10.1 is a breakdown of potential sources where some of the information noted can be obtained for any geographic area.

Exhibit 10.1 Potential Source Data on Population, Consumer Spending, and Employment

---

Population and Demographic Characteristics:

U.S. Census of Population and Housing

Kind of data:	Demographics, housing, population, incomes.
Geography covered:	U.S., states, census tracts, zip codes, and block data.
Frequency:	Every 10 years for comprehensive census data. After 2000 the census bureau started the American Community Survey (ACS). This program is a comprehensive effort by the bureau to replace the long form, which was administered to one in seven people during the decennial census, with data from annual large-sample survey. This survey provides current annualized data for all areas with 65,000 or more persons, annual data based on three-year averages for areas with between 20,000 and 65,000 persons, and annual data based on five-year averages for areas as small as individual census tracts. Data at the tract level will not be available until 2010 and then annually thereafter. Other statistics like county- and MSA-level data are already available for many areas. *Source:* U.S. Bureau of the Census (www.census.gov).

Buying Power, Consumer Spending:

Bureau of Labor Statistics—Consumer Expenditure Survey

Kind of data:	Consumer spending.
Covered:	Regional, MSA for major cities.
Frequency:	Biennially.
Source:	U.S. Department of Labor, Bureau of Labor Statistics (www.bls.gov/cex)
Content:	The survey indicates how much households (BLS uses the term "consumer units") spent for major items such as housing, transportation, retail spending, health, savings, education, and insurance. Subgroup detail data for each group are available.
Methodology:	
Diary Survey	Consumer units complete a record of expenses for two consecutive one-week periods.
Interview Survey	An interviewer visits each of the consumer units in the sample every three months over a 12-month period. The expenditures are based on consumer recall for the period. The results of these two surveys are reconciled into the final report.

Annual Retail Trade Survey

Kind of data:	Retail establishment sales, number of establishments, annual payroll.
Covered:	U.S., state, county, MSA, city, and zip code.

(*continued*)

Exhibit 10.1   (Continued)

Frequency:	Every five years, years ending in 02 and 07.
Source:	U.S. Bureau of the Census (www.census.gov/econ).
Content:	Retail sales by seven-digit NAICS code, number of establishments, and payroll. The report, released each spring, contains estimates of annual sales, per capita sales, gross margins, monthly and year-end inventories, and sales/inventory ratios by kind of business.
Methodology:	A mandatory survey of all major business establishments and sample survey of small businesses.

Employment:
County Business Patterns

Kind of data:	Employment.
Covered:	States and counties.
Frequency:	Annual.
Source:	U.S. Census Bureau (www.census.gov/epcd/cbp).
Content:	The series provides employment data by county, both current and historical. The series excludes data on self-employed individuals, employees of private households, railroads employees, agricultural production employees, and most governmental employees.

Bureau of Labor Statistics

Kind of data:	Employment data (usually the most current).
Covered:	U.S., states, counties, and some MSAs. The data are only for workers covered by federal unemployment insurance, so they exclude many categories such as the government and armed services.
Source:	www.bls.gov/cew

State Agency—Employment and Wages by Industry and County

Kind of data:	Employment, income, earnings.
Covered:	States and counties.
Frequency:	Quarterly, semiannually—varies from state to state.
Source:	State Department of Labor or Employment Commission. Offices of these departments exist in each state. Statistics are compiled by at least one of these agencies and sometimes by both.
Content:	Varies from state to state but generally the data will cover monthly employment and earnings by industry group.
Methodology:	Typically data are compiled from quarterly contribution and wage reports submitted by employers subject to the State Unemployment Compensation Act.

Source: Stephen Fanning, *Market Analysis for Real Estate* (Chicago: Appraisal Institute, 2005), p. 152.

11

REAL ESTATE VALUATION AND INVESTMENT ANALYSIS

WHAT IS REAL ESTATE VALUATION?

Real estate valuation is the key to investment in the real estate market. Valuation answers the question: How much is this property worth today? Investors use different types of analysis and procedures to determine the valuation of a particular piece of property.

Market value of a real estate asset is commonly defined as "the most probable price which a property should bring in a competitive and open market under all conditions requisite to a fair sale, the buyer and seller each acting prudently and knowledgeably, and assuming the price is not affected by undue stimulus."[1] Valuation helps estimate the price at which the buyer could be willing to buy and the seller could be willing to sell. Obviously it is not uncommon for the buyer and the seller to come up with different values for the same asset. The seller most likely comes up with a value on the higher end of the range while the buyer comes up with a value at the lower end of the range. However, there is always that price at which the asset would be sold by well-informed, willing, and able buyers and sellers. Real estate valuation helps the parties come to this price quicker and avoids wasting time in the negotiations.

---

1. William B. Brueggeman and Jeffrey D. Fisher, *Real Estate Finance and Investments,* 12th ed. (New York: McGraw-Hill Irwin, 2005), p. 255.

A very important concept in real estate asset valuation is that investors' expected return has an inverse relationship to the price of the asset. This inverse relationship exists because in a real estate valuation model, the future cash flow of the asset, which is made up of the annual income and the estimated reversion price, remains constant regardless of what the investor pays today.

APPROACHES TO REAL ESTATE VALUATION

There are three common approaches used in real estate valuation in practice:

1. Income approach

2. Sales comparison approach

3. Costs approach

Income Approach

The underlying concept of the income approach to real estate valuation is that the asset's value is based on its income-producing ability. This approach is commonly used in commercial property valuation and uses the existing lease information in addition to market rates in determining value. The two commonly used income approaches in the industry are discounted cash flow (DCF) and direct capitalization.

Discounted Cash Flow   Discounted cash flow is the most widely used method in the determination of value in commercial real estate transactions. It is based on the present value of future cash flows. Future cash flows, which are made up of the annual income and the resale price, are discounted to their value today. The annual income commonly used is the property's net operating income (NOI). In practice, investors usually use a property's 10-year cash flow with reversion at the end of year 10 in a DCF valuation. Under this method, future vacancies and renewal probabilities are estimated for leases that would expire within the 10-year period.

The three steps in a discounted cash flow valuation are:

1. Forecast the property's future NOI.

2. Select a discount rate.

3. Discount the NOI to present value using the discount rate or required internal rate of return.

Forecasting the NOI   To get to the forecasted NOI, you first need to forecast the revenues, vacancies, credit losses, and expenses. It is important to note that capital expenditures, depreciations, and amortizations are not factored in determining NOI. In general, capital improvements are excluded. Also, depreciation and amortizations are excluded because they are noncash transactions used in accounting to record the wear and tear of capital assets over time.

A sample 10-year forecast of NOI is shown in Exhibit 11.1.

It is important is note that the effective gross income (EGI) is used instead of the potential gross income (PGI). PGI is made up of all the forecasted revenue of the property without adjusting for vacancies and credit loss due to tenant default. Therefore, PGI would include these revenue items:

Rents from current tenants

Market rents from lease renewals

Parking revenues

Antenna space rental revenues

Billboard advertising

Miscellaneous other rental income

EGI is the potential gross income adjusted for forecasted vacancies and credit losses. EGI is also the forecasted income prior to the deduction of expenses in arriving at the NOI.

Discount Rates   After determining the forecasted NOI over the holding period, these NOIs would be discounted to their present values. The question here is what discount rate should be used in discounting these NOIs. It is important to note that a minor difference in the discount rate can yield a significantly different value, so care should be taken in using an appropriate discount rate. The discount rate used should be thought of as a required return for a similar real estate investment with similar risk and returns in that particular market. Therefore, an analyst or investor performing this type of analysis needs to ensure that the appropriate discount rate is used.

Discount the NOI Using the Discount Rate   After the NOIs and the discount rate are determined, the next step is to discount the NOIs to their present values. Let us assume that it was determined that 5.25 percent is an appropriate discount rate based on the risk, nature of the asset, and market condition. Also since the investor intends to hold the asset for 10 years, the analysis in year 10 will need to show the reversion value.

Using the data from Exhibit 11.1, the DCF over the 10-year holding period would be as indicated in Exhibit 11.2.

Exhibit 11.1 Projected Net Operating Income

	Year 1	Year 2	Year 3	Year 4	Year 5	Year 6	Year 7	Year 8	Year 9	Year 10
REVENUES:										
Rent from existing leases	1,000,000	1,050,000	1,100,000	1,005,000	1,100,000	1,250,000	1,300,000	1,380,000	1,300,000	1,500,000
Projected market rent from lease renewal	—	—	—	100,000	105,000	—	—	—	110,000	—
Parking revenue	200,000	200,000	210,000	220,000	250,000	255,000	255,000	260,000	260,000	300,000
Antenna rental	50,000	50,000	50,000	50,000	50,000	60,000	60,000	60,000	60,000	60,000
Potential Gross Income (PGI)	1,250,000	1,300,000	1,360,000	1,375,000	1,505,000	1,565,000	1,615,000	1,700,000	1,730,000	1,860,000
Forecasted vacancies	62,500	65,000	68,000	68,750	75,250	78,250	80,750	85,000	86,500	93,000
Forecasted credit loss	50,000	52,000	54,400	55,000	60,200	62,600	64,600	68,000	69,200	74,400
Effective Gross Income (EGI)	1,137,500	1,183,000	1,237,600	1,251,250	1,369,550	1,424,150	1,469,650	1,547,000	1,574,300	1,692,600
EXPENSES:										
Salaries and wages	260,000	267,800	275,834	284,109	292,632	301,411	310,454	319,767	329,360	339,241
Cleaning	15,000	15,000	15,000	20,000	20,000	20,000	20,000	25,000	25,000	25,000
Utilities	12,000	12,480	12,979	13,498	14,038	14,600	15,184	15,791	16,423	17,080
Repairs and maintenance	10,000	10,400	10,816	11,249	11,699	12,167	12,653	13,159	13,686	14,233
Management fees	50,000	52,000	54,400	55,000	60,200	62,600	64,600	68,000	69,200	74,400
Insurance	13,000	13,520	14,061	14,623	15,208	15,816	16,449	17,107	17,791	18,503
Property taxes	230,550	239,772	249,363	259,337	269,711	280,499	291,719	303,388	315,524	328,145
Office supplies	9,000	9,360	9,734	10,124	10,529	10,950	11,388	11,843	12,317	12,810
Miscellaneous expenses	8,000	8,000	8,000	10,000	10,000	10,000	12,000	12,000	12,000	14,000
Total Expenses	607,550	628,332	650,187	677,940	704,017	728,043	754,447	786,056	811,301	843,411
Net Operating Income (NOI)	529,950	554,668	587,413	573,310	665,533	696,107	715,203	760,944	762,999	849,189

Exhibit 11.2 Discounted Net Operating Income

						Years					
	1	2	3	4	5	6	7	8	9	10	11
REVENUES:											
Rent from existing leases	1,000,000	1,050,000	1,100,000	1,005,000	1,100,000	1,250,000	1,300,000	1,380,000	1,300,000	1,500,000	1,600,000
Projected market rent from lease renewal	—	—	—	100,000	105,000	—	—	—	110,000	—	—
Parking revenue	200,000	200,000	210,000	220,000	250,000	255,000	255,000	260,000	260,000	300,000	300,000
Antenna rental	50,000	50,000	50,000	50,000	50,000	60,000	60,000	60,000	60,000	60,000	60,000
Potential Gross Income (PGI)	1,250,000	1,300,000	1,360,000	1,375,000	1,505,000	1,565,000	1,615,000	1,700,000	1,730,000	1,860,000	1,960,000
Forecasted vacancies	62,500	65,000	68,000	68,750	75,250	78,250	80,750	85,000	86,500	93,000	98,000
Forecasted credit loss	50,000	52,000	54,400	55,000	60,200	62,600	64,600	68,000	69,200	74,400	78,400
Effective Gross Income (EGI)	1,137,500	1,183,000	1,237,600	1,251,250	1,369,550	1,424,150	1,469,650	1,547,000	1,574,300	1,692,600	1,783,600
EXPENSES:											
Salaries and wages	260,000	267,800	275,834	284,109	292,632	301,411	310,454	319,767	329,360	339,241	349,418
Cleaning	15,000	15,000	15,000	20,000	20,000	20,000	20,000	25,000	25,000	25,000	25,000
Utilities	12,000	12,480	12,979	13,498	14,038	14,600	15,184	15,791	16,423	17,080	17,763
Repairs and maintenance	10,000	10,400	10,816	11,249	11,699	12,167	12,653	13,159	13,686	14,233	14,802
Management fees	50,000	52,000	54,400	55,000	60,200	62,600	64,600	68,000	69,200	74,400	78,400
Insurance	13,000	13,520	14,061	14,623	15,208	15,816	16,449	17,107	17,791	18,503	19,243
Property taxes	230,550	239,772	249,363	259,337	269,711	280,499	291,719	303,388	315,524	328,145	341,270
Office supplies	9,000	9,360	9,734	10,124	10,529	10,950	11,388	11,843	12,317	12,810	13,322
Miscellaneous expenses	8,000	8,000	8,000	10,000	10,000	10,000	12,000	12,000	12,000	14,000	14,000
Total Expenses	607,550	628,332	650,187	677,940	704,017	728,043	754,447	786,056	811,301	843,411	873,219
Net Operating Income (NOI)	529,950	554,668	587,413	573,310	665,533	696,107	715,203	760,944	762,999	849,189	910,381
Reversion Value (using 6% terminal cap rate)										14,173,011	
Total Cash Flow	529,950	554,668	587,413	573,310	665,533	696,107	715,203	760,944	762,999	15,022,200	
Discount Rate	5.25%										
Discounted Cash Flow	503,515	500,713	503,822	467,198	515,299	512,086	499,890	505,331	481,421	9,005,597	
Property Value	$ 13,494,872										

111

The reversion value usually is determined based on the forecasted NOI of the year after the projected holding period. The reversion value used in Exhibit 11.2 is determined as:

Forecasted yr 11 NOI	$ 910,381	A
Terminal cap rate	6%	B
Reversion value	$15,173,017	C = A/B
Selling costs	(1,000,000)	
Net reversion value	$14,173,017	

Even in cases where an investor plans to hold the asset for more than 10 years, instead of running this analysis for, say, the 30 years that the investor plans to hold the asset, the terminal cap rate. Therefore, the terminal cap rate is used to approximate the present value of the asset's cash flow for the remaining holding period or economic life. Empirically, terminal capitalization rate is calculated as the discount rate minus the long-term expected growth rate.

Direct Capitalization   The direct capitalization method is a quick and easy method of calculating the estimated value of a property. This method is appropriate for income-producing properties and also can be used as an alternative check for the value determined using the discounted NOI method. The direct capitalization rate is commonly called the cap rate. Under this method, the property value is determined using this simple calculation:

Value = NOI/Capitalization Rate

The NOI used in this calculation is the stabilized NOI of the property, and the capitalization rate used should be based on recent transactions for similar properties in the market where the subject property is located. The properties examined should be alike in quality, size, age, improvements, location, functionality, operating and engineering efficiencies, tenant composition, and lease terms, among others. However, differences in these factors should be considered in determining the appropriate rate. The analyst or investor would have to use a cap rate from a property that is most similar to the subject property and adjust for differences. One of the downsides of using the cap rate for valuations is that the value is determined based on only one year's NOI; therefore, it does not consider the asset's cash flow after year 1. Determining an asset's value based on the cap rate alone could be problematic and could lead to an incorrect valuation.

Example

Assume a 200,000-square-foot office space in downtown Canton, Ohio, with year-1 NOI of $1,200,000 is offered for sale. The market cap rate for similar properties in that market is determined to be approximately 6%.

Using this information, the estimated value would be:

Value = NOI/Cap rate

$= \$1,200,000/6\%$

$= \$20,000,000$

It is very important to make sure that an appropriate cap rate is used due to its significant impact on the valuation. A half-percent difference can have a major impact on the value calculated.

Example

Assume the same information as in the prior section except that the cap rate is now determined to be 5.5% instead of 6.6%. The new value would be:

Value = NOI/Cap Rate

$= 1,200,000/5.5\%$

$= \$21,818,182$

Thus a $\frac{1}{2}$-point difference results in a valuation difference of $1,818,182.

Sales Comparison Approach

The sales comparison approach is used predominantly in the valuation of one- and two-family residential properties. This approach is used in these cases because characteristics of a property other than income are used in determining value. The estimated value of the subject property is determined by comparing the subject property to recent similar properties sold in that market. The sales comparison approach is based on the premise that similar properties in the same geographic area are sold at prices comparable to each other. The properties used in the comparison should be recent transactions that were at arm's length. They should also be transactions between parties with reasonable knowledge of the properties and market. The comparable properties should not be forced sales or transactions between related parties.

During sales comparison, the analysis focuses on the similarities and differences that affect value. These factors include but are not limited to:

- Property rights appraised
- The motivations of buyers and sellers

- Financing terms

- Market conditions at the time of sale

- Size

- Location

- Physical features

- Economic characteristics, if the properties produce income

- Age of the property[2]

These characteristics are then compared between the subject property and the comparable properties. In estimating the subject property value the differences between the subject property and each of the comparable properties are adjusted on the comparable properties sales value in determining value for the subject property.

In determining a subject property's value using the sale comparison approach, five fundamental procedures are used:

1. Research the competitive market for information on sales transactions, listings, and offers to purchase or sell involving properties that are similar to the subject property in terms of characteristics such as property type, date of sale, size, physical condition, location, and land use constraints. The goal is to find a set of comparable sales as similar as possible to the subject property.

2. Verify the information by confirming that the data obtained are factually accurate and that the transactions reflect arm's-length market considerations. Verification may elicit additional information about the market.

3. Select relevant units of comparison (e.g., price per acre, price per square foot, price per front foot) and develop a comparative analysis for each unit. The goal here is to define and identify a unit of comparison that explains market behavior.

4. Look for differences between the comparable sale properties and the subject property using the elements of comparison. Then adjust the price of each sale property to reflect how it differs from the subject property or eliminate that property as a comparable. This step typically involves using the most comparable sale properties and then adjusting for any remaining differences.

---

2. The Appraisal Institute, *The Appraisal of Real Estate*, 12th ed. (Chicago: Author, 2001), p. 417.

5. Reconcile the various value indications produced from the analysis of comparables into a single value indication or a range of values.[3]

A simplified sample sales comparison valuation for a one-family home with three similar recent sales in the same geographic area as the subject property is shown in Exhibit 11.3.

After each of the comparables is adjusted based on its similarities and differences with the subject property, a range of values is obtained for the subject property. After the adjustments, the range of values obtained from each of the comparable properties provides a reasonable estimate of the subject property's market value. In the example shown in Exhibit 11.3, the price range was from $252,500 to $262,000, with average price of the three properties $257,900.

Cost Approach

The cost approach is another method used in the valuation of real estate. This method is based on the assumption that investors look at the fair value of real estate as the cost to develop a new or a substitute property similar to the subject property, adjusted for differences such as age, physical condition, and functional utility. For the cost approach, the cost to develop a new or substitute property is determined based on current costs to replace the building. After the determination of this current cost, the amount is adjusted for functional wear and tear of the subject property. This is known as depreciation. Another way to look at the cost approach is that the fair market value is equal to market value of the land plus the cost of improvement for a similar but new property adjusted for physical and functional depreciation. These costs are obtained through market research.

In a cost approach, certain fundamental steps are necessary in determining the property's value. These steps are:

1. Estimate the value of the land as though vacant and available to be developed to its highest and best use.

2. Determine which cost basis is most applicable to the assignment: reproduction cost or replacement cost.

3. Estimate the direct (hard) and indirect (soft) costs of the improvements as of the effective appraisal date.

4. Estimate an appropriate entrepreneurial profit or incentive from analysis of the market.

5. Add estimated direct costs, indirect costs, and entrepreneurial profit or incentive to arrive at the total cost of the improvements.

---

3. Ibid., p. 422.

Exhibit 11.3 Simplified Sales Comparison Analysis

Characteristics	Subject Property	Comparable Property 1	Comparable Property 2	Comparable Property 3
Property rights	Fee Simple	Fee Simple	Fee Simple	Fee Simple
Conditions of sale	Arm's-length transaction	Arm's-length transaction	Arm's-length transaction	Arm's-length transaction
Financing terms	Cash	Cash	Loan assumed by seller	Cash
Market conditions	Current	Three months ago	Current	A year ago
Size	2,500 square feet	2,100 square feet	2,000 square feet	2,500 square feet
Location	Quiet street and walking distance to neighborhood shopping center	Same	Same	Better location
Physical features	Average	Requires upgrades	Average	Average
Age	30 years	40 years	15 years	15 years
Adjustments:				
Price		$ 200,000	$ 260,000	$ 275,000
Property rights	$ —	$ —	$ —	$ —
Conditions of sale	$ —	$ —	$ —	$ —
Financing terms	$ —	$ —	$ (10,000)	$ —
Market conditions	$ —	$ 4,000	$ —	$ 19,250
Size	$ —	$ 18,000	$ 22,500	$ —
Location	$ —	$ —	$ —	$ (15,000)
Physical features	$ —	$ 25,000	$ —	$ —
Age	$ —	$ 15,000	$ (20,000)	$ (20,000)
Total adjustments	$ —	$ 62,000	$ (7,500)	$ (15,750)
Adjusted price		**$ 262,000**	**$ 252,500**	**$ 259,250**
Estimated value (average)	**$ 257,917**			

6. Estimate the amount of depreciation in the structure and, if necessary, allocate it among the three major categories:

   ○ Physical deterioration

   ○ Functional obsolescence

   ○ External obsolescence

7. Deduct estimated depreciation from the total cost of the improvements to derive an estimate of their depreciated cost.

8. Estimate the contributory value of any site improvements that have not already been considered. (Site improvements are often appraised at their contributory value—i.e., directly on a depreciated-cost basis— but may be included in the overall cost calculated in Step 2.)

9. Add land value to the total depreciated cost of all the improvements to arrive at the indicated value of the property.

10. Adjust the indicated value of the property for any personal property (e.g., furniture, fixtures, and equipment) or any intangible asset value that may be included in the cost estimate. If necessary, this value, which reflects the value of the fee simple interest, may be adjusted for the property interest being appraised to arrive at the indicated value of the specified interest in the property.[4]

---

4. Ibid., p. 356.

12

FINANCING OF REAL ESTATE

Investment in real estate requires significant capital. Investors therefore often look outside their own firms to the capital market to raise the funds to invest in these assets. Even investors who have the funds available might not want to put up the whole amount but prefer to use leverage. The two most common ways investors can use to fund the purchase of real estate are equity and debt financing.

EQUITY

Equity investment includes the investor's own capital and capital from other investors in the purchase of the real estate. The investors could be individual investors, partnerships of individuals or corporations, investments clubs, private equity funds, hedge funds, investment banks, commercial banks, and pension funds, among others. In an equity investment funding structure the investors share the risks and rewards of the real estate investment. The return for these investors would include periodic cash flow from the investment and gains upon disposal of the assts.

DEBT FINANCING

The focus of this chapter is debt financing of real estate. Debt financing can be obtained through numerous sources. Eight of the most common lenders are:

1. Commercial banks
2. Investment banks

3. Mortgage banks

4. Credit unions

5. Pension funds

6. Life insurance firms

7. Savings and loan associations

8. Mortgage real estate investment trusts

Commercial Banks

Commercial banks usually are chartered by the federal or state governments in which the banks operate. Real estate financing is one of many avenues through which commercial banks invest deposits from their customers. Traditionally, because of the short-term nature of customer deposits, commercial banks offer both short-term and long-term financing. Deposits of bank customers are usually insured up to a limit provided by the Federal Deposit Insurance Corporation (FDIC), which is currently up to $250,000. Examples of commercial banks in the United States include Citibank, Bank of America, and JP Morgan Chase.

Investment Banks

Investment banks operate mostly in the capital market. These banks help their customers raise significant money in the capital market through debt and equity offerings. They are located mainly in major financial cities and have global networks of offices. They help in the financing of multimillion- and billion-dollar real estate transaction across nations. As a result of the 2008 financial crisis and subsequent bailout of most banks by the U.S. government, most banks that were investment banks converted to commercial banks. So now the delineation between commercial and investment banks is no longer as clear as it used to be. Examples of former investment banks that converted to commercial banks include Goldman Sachs and Morgan Stanley, among others. Some commercial banks also have investment banking divisions that perform similar investment banking transactions.

Mortgage Banks

Unlike other banks that provide real estate and other investment services, mortgage banks focus on real estate financing. These banks originate loans for both themselves and their clients (which include commercial banks, investment banks, life insurance firms, pension funds, and others). When mortgage banks originate loans for themselves, they hold the mortgage until maturity, thereby keeping the mortgages on their own books. They earn fees for originating loans for clients, and they earn service fees if they are the servicing agent on the loan. (Servicing means collecting the periodic mortgage payments from borrowers and remitting them to the lender.) Most mortgage banks are chartered by the state. There are numerous mortgage banks in every state in the United States.

Credit Unions

Credit unions are cooperative organizations that make loans to members. Members make deposits with the credit union and are paid interest on their deposits. Members also can borrow from credit unions for personal use. One of the benefits of credit unions is that the interest they charge members is usually lower than most members can obtain from other sources; thus, most members borrow from the credit union when they purchase real estate.

Life Insurance Firms

Life insurance firms obtain cash through the premiums from policy holders and returns on investments. The cash is then used to cover claims and operating costs. Real estate represents a major asset class for most life insurance firms due to the fairly predictable nature of real estate cash flow. Most of these insurance firms invest on both the equity and debt sides of real estate. Some of these insurance firms such as American International Group (AIG) invest in real estate–related equity and debt derivatives such as credit default swaps (CDS). These derivatives resulted in the near collapse or total collapse of AIG, ACA Capital, Lehman Brothers, Merrill Lynch, and similar other firms during the 2008 financial crisis.

Savings and Loan Associations

Savings and loan associations are chartered by state or federal laws. They lend only to their members, normally for long-term financing of home purchases. The savings and loans association industry went through a near collapse in the late 1980s and early 1990s due to bad loans until it was rescued by the federal government. Savings and loans associations currently are regulated by the Federal Home Loan Bank (FHLB) system, a federal regulatory agency that sets guidelines and provides depositors with insurance protection for deposits under the Federal Savings and Loan Insurance Corporation.

Mortgage Real Estate Investment Trusts

Real estate investment trusts (REITs) were defined and authorized by the U.S. Congress in the Real Estate Investment Trust Act of 1960. The purpose of the act was to provide individual investors with the opportunity to participate in owning and/or financing a diversified portfolio of real estate.

There are three main types of REITs: mortgage REITs, equity REITs, and hybrid REITs. Mortgage REITs provide and hold loans and other bond-like obligations that are secured by real estate collateral. Equity REITs invest in real estate through the purchase of equity interests. Hybrid REITs invest in both real estate equity and debt interests. The main benefit of REITs as an investment vehicle is that the investors avoid double taxation.

OTHER FINANCING SOURCES

Over the years, many complex financial instruments have been created as sources of financing real estate investments. Three of the most common ones are:

1. Mezzanine debt

2. Preferred equity financing

3. Collateralized mortgage obligations

Mezzanine Debt

Mezzanine debt (also called mezzanine loan or "mezz" for short) is a loan to the equity investor in debt-financed real estate. The mezzanine loan is secured by the borrower's equity interest in the real estate asset. Mezzanine loans were created to provide additional financing to equity investors.

Preferred Equity Financing

Preferred equity financing is very similar to a mezzanine loan because it is also provided to the equity investor. However, in a preferred equity financing, the preferred equity investor is entitled to receive all or a portion of the borrower's excess cash flow from the investment until the preferred equity holder's investment is repaid in addition to an agreed-on return. A preferred equity investment is more secure than a common equity investment in the event of dissolution.

Collateralized Mortgage Obligations

Collateralized mortgage obligations (CMOs) were created to help convert the cash flow from real estate mortgages into various investment instruments that fit the needs of particular investors. CMOs are essentially bonds sold to investors that are secured by mortgage cash flows. CMOs are structured, packaged, and sold by some of the major banks to sophisticated investors and firms. In principle, according to Davidson and coauthors, "The mortgage cash flows are distributed to the bond[holders] based on a set of pre-specified rules and the rules determine the order of principal allocation and the coupon level."[1]

TYPES OF LOANS

In general, there are two main broad types of loan: conventional and guaranteed loans.

Conventional Loans

In conventional loans, the risk of the lender not being able to recover its investment depends on the borrower's ability to pay its debt obligations and also the availability of sufficient equity in the financed asset in the event of the borrower's default. In conventional loans, there are no guarantees provided by any other third party. Due to the risks involved, lenders tend to require larger down payments in order to reduce the loan to value so that in event of default by the borrower, the lender would be more likely to recover its investment.

Guaranteed Loans

Guaranteed loans are insured or guaranteed by another party other than the borrower. Some of the most common guaranteed loans are those guaranteed by the government or its agencies, such as Federal Housing Authority–insured loans, Veteran's Administration–guaranteed loans, and Small Business Administration–guaranteed loans. Depending on the agency that insured or guaranteed the loan, different percentages of the loan are guaranteed.

DEBT AGREEMENTS

In a debt-financed real estate purchase, buyers usually pledge their ownership interests in the investment as collateral for the debt used in purchasing the real estate asset. In some cases, depending on the risks involved, buyers might be required to personally guarantee the debt, meaning that if cash flow from the investment is not adequate to satisfy the debt obligation, the buyer would personally fulfill the obligation.

---

1. Andrew Davidson, Anthony Sanders, Lan-Ling Wolff, and Anne Ching, *Securitization: Structuring and Investment Analysis* (Hoboken, NJ: John Wiley & Sons, 2003), p. 185.

In a debt financing, the borrower and the lender normally formalize their rights and obligations through an executed loan agreement. A typical loan agreement would normally contain the following terms:

- Loan amount
- Interest rate
- Down payment
- Loan service payment
- Loan maturity date
- Early repayment option
- Loan default
- Recourse
- Nonrecourse
- Renewal option
- Closing costs
- Loan assignment
- Guaranty

Loan Amount

Loan amount means the principal amount borrowed from the lender(s). Depending on how the loan is structured, if periodic loan service payments include principal and interest, the loan balance decreases with every loan service payment.

Interest Rate

Interest rate is the cost of borrowing money from the lender. Interest rates are expressed per annum and usually negotiated between the borrower and the lender. The amount of interest is based on the expected risk of the investment and the creditworthiness of the borrower. Interest rates can be fixed or variable, depending on the loan structure that is agreed to between the parties.

Down Payment

A down payment is the initial deposit made by the borrower at the time of signing the loan agreement. Lenders usually require borrowers to put up a reasonable down payment to ensure that the borrower has money at risk in the transaction. The down payment ensures that the borrower has a financial interest in the transaction and therefore could not easily walk away from the deal. In case of default, it also increases the likelihood that the lender would be able to recover its money since the lender ordinarily finances the difference between the purchase price and the down payment.

Loan Service Payment

The loan service payment represents the periodic payment by the borrower to the lender for the use of the lender's money. These payments can be monthly, quarterly, semiannually, or annually, depending on the agreement between the parties. The loan service may be interest-only or principal-plus-interest payments.

Other loan service arrangements exist, such as negative amortization and periodic future lump-sum payments. In a negative amortization, the periodic loan service payment is less than the interest cost; thus the loan balance increases periodically instead of decreasing. For a future lump-sum payment arrangement, at predetermined points during the loan period, the borrower will make lump-sum payments toward reduction of loan balance. Fully amortized loans have equal payments made up of principal and interest such that at the end of the loan period, the loan balance is zero.

Loan Maturity Date

The loan maturity date is the date on which the loan balance is either paid off or due to the lender. In a fully amortized loan, the loan balance is zero on the loan maturity date. If the loan is not a fully amortized loan, the balance is paid off on the loan maturity date.

Early Repayment Option

The early repayment option is the borrower's right under the loan agreement to repay the loan at any time prior to the loan maturity date. The parties can agree whether prior notice or an early repayment penalty is required before a borrower can repay the loan prior to the maturity date.

Loan Default

A loan default is the borrower's failure to fulfill its obligations under the terms of the loan. An act of default could include nonpayment or late payment of the periodic loan service payments. In some cases, borrowers can be in default if the note specifies the condition in which the asset should be maintained to retain its value. Thus, if the borrower fails to fulfill this obligation, it is in violation of the loan agreement. It is important to understand that a default is not only a nonpayment or late payment issue but could include other violations as specified in the loan agreement.

Recourse

Recourse is a loan provision that holds the investor personally liable in the event of loan default. This means that the lender has the right to go after the borrower's personal assets in event of a default.

Nonrecourse

Nonrecourse is the opposite of recourse. In case of a default, the lender can recover the amount of loan due only from the asset used as collateral for the loan. On a nonrecourse loan, the lender cannot hold the borrower personally responsible in the event of default.

Renewal Option

For certain loans that are not fully amortized, the loan agreement may give the borrower the right to renew the loan for a certain length of time after the original maturity date. If the borrower has this right, the loan agreement will specify the amount of time prior to the original maturity date at which the borrower will notify the lender of the intent to renew the loan. The agreement will also specify the conditions under which the lender can grant the borrower the right to renew. Some conditions may include certain performance criteria. One of the benefits of a renewal option is that it saves the borrower certain costs, such as loan closing costs, that could have to be spent if the borrower was to refinance the debt with another lender.

Closing Costs

Closing costs are the costs usually incurred by the borrower in obtaining a loan. Some examples of closing costs are origination fees, application fees, loan points, and recording fees.

Loan Assignment

Loan assignment is the lender's right under the loan agreement to sell the note to another party without any prior approval from the borrower. However, the borrower should be informed to ensure that payments and notices are sent to the appropriate party.

Guaranty

A guaranty is a legal document that obligates one party to pay the debt of another party in event of default. For example, a parent company can be required to sign an agreement that says that in the event of default by its subsidiary, the parent company will be liable to fulfill the loan obligations. Most lenders require guaranty in cases where the financial stability of the borrower is in question.

FINANCING COSTS

Real estate transactions involve significant costs to obtain the financing and prepare the loan documents. Most of these costs are paid by the borrower. In a few cases, though, they are paid by the lender; however, they are somehow recovered from the borrower. Six of the most common financing costs are:

1. Application fee
2. Origination fee
3. Broker's commission
4. Loan points
5. Transfer taxes
6. Legal fees

Application Fee

The application fee is the amount charged by the lender to process the borrower's loan application. This amount varies by lender and can be negotiated.

Origination Fee

The origination fee is the amount paid by the borrower to the lender for providing the loan. The amount varies by lender and can be negotiated between the parties. The lender charges this fee for its service in sourcing the loan.

Broker's Commission

In some cases, the borrower might go through a mortgage broker to obtain the loan. The broker may be compensated by either the lender or the borrower; however, the fee paid to the broker is called the broker's commission. This amount varies and can be as little as 0.5 percent to as much as 3 percent of the loan amount.

Loan Points

Loan points basically are an additional fee charged by the lender to the borrower for providing the loan. Each point represents 1 percent of the loan amount. Points might vary depending on the risks and the borrower's credit history.

Transfer Taxes

Transfer taxes are paid to the municipal government where the property is located. The amount is determined by the municipal government in the area. The actual transfer tax paid is based on the loan amount.

Legal Fees

Loan documents are usually drafted by the lender's attorney and submitted to the borrower and/or the borrower's attorney to concur with the terms of the loan. A borrower normally needs an attorney to review the terms and language to ensure that its interests are adequately protected and that the terms are what the parties agreed to. The fees for the attorney's service are called legal fees or attorney fees.

RELATIONSHIP BETWEEN A NOTE AND A MORTGAGE

A mortgage is a legal document that evidences that a property is encumbered by a loan obligation. It serves as the lender's security interest in the debt-financed real property. A mortgage is normally executed contemporaneously with the note. A note, which is the loan agreement, obligates the borrower to repay the loan in accordance with the terms agreed to by the parties. The mortgage secures the lender's interest in the financing and gives the lender the right to sue in an event of default by the borrower.

ACCOUNTING FOR FINANCING COSTS

The financing costs described in this chapter are incurred as a result of debt financing of a real estate purchase. These costs would not have been incurred if the purchase were not financed with debt. Generally accepted accounting principles require that these costs should be capitalized and amortized as an expense over the loan term on a straight-line basis.

Example

If the total financing costs for a real estate transaction were $10,000 for a 10-year loan, the $10,000 should be capitalized on the borrower's balance sheet. Then each year $1,000 ($10,000/10 years) should be expensed.

13

ACCOUNTING FOR REAL ESTATE INVESTMENTS AND ACQUISITION COSTS

As discussed in Chapter 3, there are different forms of real estate entities in practice, including general partnerships, limited partnerships, corporate joint ventures, undivided interests, and public and private real estate investment trusts (REITs). Each entity differs in legal formation and economic substance. The accounting and reporting of investments in any of these forms of ownership vary significantly.

METHODS OF ACCOUNTING FOR REAL ESTATE INVESTMENTS

Real estate investments, like other types of investments, must be accounted and reported using four principal methods:

1. Cost method
2. Equity method
3. Fair market value method
4. Consolidation method

Cost Method

The cost method of accounting and reporting is the method in which the investor records and recognizes its ownership interest in the investee at cost and then records as income dividends received from the net accumulated retained earnings of the investee since the investment by the investor. Under this method, only the dividend distributed by the investee company is recognized by the investor as income on the investor's books. If at any point the investee distributes to investors more than the net accumulated retained earnings, the investor would need to recognize its share of the cumulative distribution in excess of net accumulated retained earnings as a return of capital.

Because under the cost method dividends are the only basis for recognizing income on the investor's books, this method does not timely reflect the income of the investee on the investor's books; thus, income recognized by the investee in one accounting period might not be reflected in the investor's book until many subsequent periods later. This is one reason why the cost method has limited use in real estate. In practice, the cost method can be used by a limited partner with a minor interest in a partnership where the limited partner has no influence over the partnership's operating and financial activities.

Equity Method

The equity method is a very popular method for accounting and reporting real estate investments, especially when there are two or more investors in the ownership of real estate or real estate development projects. Under the equity method, an investor initially records an investment in the stock of an investee at cost and adjusts the carrying amount of the investment to recognize the investor's share of the earnings or losses of the investee after the date of acquisition.[1] The amount of the adjustment is included in the determination of net income by the investor. The amount reflects adjustments similar to those made in preparing consolidated statements, including adjustments to eliminate intercompany gains and losses and to amortize, if appropriate, any difference between investor cost and the investee's underlying equity in net assets at the date of investment. The investor's investment is also adjusted to reflect its share of changes in the investee's capital. Dividends received from an investee reduce the carrying amount of the investment.

Under the equity method, an investor recognizes its share of the earnings or losses of an investee in the periods for which they are reported by the investee in its financial statements rather than in the period in which an investee declares a dividend.[2] An investor adjusts the carrying amount of an investment for its share of the earnings or losses of the investee subsequent to the date of investment and reports the recognized earnings or losses in income. Dividends received from an investee reduce the carrying amount

---

1. American Institute of Certified Public Accountants, APB 18, The Equity Method of Accounting for Investments in Common Stock, paragraph 6(b), 1971.
2. Ibid., paragraph 10.

of the investment. Thus, the equity method is an appropriate means of recognizing increases or decreases measured by generally accepted accounting principles in the economic resources underlying the investments. Furthermore, the equity method of accounting more closely meets the objectives of accrual accounting than does the cost method since the investor recognizes its share of the earnings and losses of the investee in the periods in which they are reflected in the investee's accounts.

Under the equity method, an investment in common stock is generally shown on the balance sheet of an investor as a single amount.[3] Likewise, an investor's share of earnings or losses from its investment is ordinarily shown on its income statement as a single amount.

The equity method is recommended and in some cases required in the accounting for real estate investments, interests in joint ventures, certain general partnerships, limited partnerships, and undivided interests. A further description of the equity method in each of these forms of ownership follows:

Corporate Joint Ventures   A corporate joint venture is a corporation owned and operated by a small group of businesses as a separate and specific business for the mutual benefit of the members of the joint venture, usually to earn a profit. The purpose of a joint venture is to share risks and rewards of the specific business. The members must have joint controls for the business to qualify as a joint venture. Investors in a joint venture are required to record their investments by the equity method of accounting.

It is important to note that a real estate entity that is a subsidiary of a joint venture should not be accounted for as a joint venture but should be accounted for by the joint venture parent using the accounting guidance applicable to investments in subsidiaries.

General Partnerships   A general partnership is a type of partnership entity in which there are only general partners. General partners are legally responsible for the actions of the business and can legally bind the business, including being personally liable for the business's debts and obligations. The liabilities of the partners in a general partnership are therefore joint and several. Investment in a noncontrolled real estate general partnership is required to be accounted for using the equity method by the investor; however, a general partnership that is controlled, whether directly or indirectly, by any of the partners should be accounted for by that partner as a subsidiary.

---

3. Ibid., paragraph 11.

Generally, "control of an entity" is defined by one of these points:

- Ownership of majority of the outstanding voting shares. "Majority" here means ownership of over 50 percent.

- Ownership of majority (over 50 percent) of the financial interests in profits and losses of the investee.

- Control power vested by contract, lease, and agreement with other partners or by court order.

However, according to AICPA Statement of Position (SOP) 78-9, *Accounting for Investments in Real Estate Ventures*, paragraph .07, the majority interest holder may not control the entity if one or more of the other partners have substantive participating rights that permit those other partners to effectively participate in significant decisions that would be expected to be made in the ordinary course of business.[4]

Limited Partnerships　In a limited partnership, the partners are made up of both general and limited partners. There is usually one or more of both general and limited partners.

Investment in a limited partnership by a limited partner is required to be accounted for using the equity method unless the limited partner's interest is minor such that the limited partner has virtually no influence, as noted under the cost method. Emerging Issues Task Force (EITF) D-46, *Accounting for Limited Partnership Investments*, notes that the Securities and Exchange Commission staff understands that practice generally has viewed investments of more than 3 to 5 percent to be more than minor.[5] Therefore, it is safe to assume that a limited partner's interest that represents more than the 3 to 5 percent range should be accounted for under the equity method. Investments not meeting this criterion would be accounted for under the cost method.

As noted in Chapter 3, the roles, rights, and obligations of the general partners are very different from those of the limited partners in a limited partnership. Generally, a sole general partner in a limited partnership is presumed to control the activities of the partnership and should consolidate the financial statement of the limited partnership with its financial statements. However according to SOP 78-9, paragraph .09:

> If the presumption of control by the general partners is overcome by the rights of the limited partners, the general partners should apply the equity method of accounting to their interests. If the presumption of control by the general

4. American Institute Certified Public Accountants (2005).
5. Financial Accounting Standards Board (Norwalk, CT,: 1995).

partners is not overcome by the rights of the limited partners and no single general partner controls the limited partnership, the general partners should apply the equity method of accounting to their interests. If the presumption of control is not overcome by the rights of the limited partners and a single general partner controls the limited partnership, that general partner should consolidate the limited partnership and apply the principles of accounting applicable for investments in subsidiaries.[6]

A general partner's control of a limited partnership can be overcome if limited partners have certain rights, namely substantive kick-out rights and substantive participating rights.

Substantive Kick-out Rights   A kick-out right is a contractual or legal right to dissolve the limited partnership or remove the general partner without cause. Whether a kick-out right of the limited partner is substantive should be based on the consideration of all the relevant facts and circumstances, such as whether the limited partner's right is based on a vote of a simple majority or if the limited partner's kick-out right has no substantial barriers.

Substantive Participating Rights   Limited partners are deemed to have a substantive participating right if they have these four rights, as provided by EITF No. 04-5, paragraph 11 (Financial Accounting Standards Board, EITF No. 04-5, *Determining Whether a General Partner, or the General Partners as a Group, Controls a Limited Partnership or Similar Entity When the Limited Partners Have Certain Rights*, Norwalk, CT, 2004):

1. Selecting, terminating, and setting the compensation of management responsible for implementing the limited partnership's policies and procedures.

2. Establishing operating and capital decisions of the limited partnership, including budgets, in the ordinary course of business.

3. The sale or refinancing of limited partnership assets.

4. The acquisition of limited partnership assets.

Fair Market Value Method

Fair market value is a method of presenting real estate investments on the books of the investor based on the investment's current readily available market value. Over the years, the real estate industry has been moving toward reporting investments based on the investment's fair market value.

---

6. Financial Accounting Standards Board, SOP 78-9, Accounting for Investments in Real Estate Venture (2005).

Proponents of this method believe that it is more representative of the investment's true value compared to the other methods.

The clearest example of reporting of fair market value is the reporting of publicly traded shares. In those markets, investors can easily determine the value of their holdings by looking up the market price of their stocks traded on one of the trading exchanges, such as the New York Stock Exchange, the American Stock Exchange, or the Nasdaq. Investors can easily determine the value of their investments. An investor would adjust the balance sheet to the current value of the investment while also reporting the change on its income statement. So, for example, if the market value of the real estate increased by $100,000, an entry would be recorded that debits the asset and credits revenue by this amount.

Currently, the fair market value method is required for all investment companies registered under the Investment Company Act of 1940.

Consolidation Method

Consolidation is the reporting of a subsidiary company's financial statements within the financial statements of the parent company. A subsidiary is an entity that is controlled, whether directly or indirectly, by another corporation. As noted under the previous general partnership discussion, the usual condition for control is ownership of a majority (over 50 percent) of the outstanding voting share. The power to control may also exist with a lesser percentage of ownership, such as by power vested under a contract, lease, or agreement with other stockholders or by court decree.

In a consolidation, a parent's and subsidiary's activities are reported as if they were one entity. Any intercompany transactions between the two entities, including gains and losses, are eliminated. Accounting Research Bulletin No. 51, *Consolidated Financial Statements*, states the purpose of consolidated financial statements in this way:

> The purpose of consolidated statements is to present, primarily for the benefit of the shareholders and creditors of the parent company, the results of operations and the financial position of a parent company and its subsidiaries essentially as if the group were a single company with one or more branches or divisions. There is a presumption that consolidated statements are more meaningful than separate statements and that they are usually necessary for a fair presentation when one of the companies in the group directly or indirectly has a controlling financial interest in the other companies.[7]

This statement clearly states the importance of consolidated financial statements, not just for the equity holders but also for the entity's debt holders.

---

7. American Institute of Certified Public Accountants (1959).

PURCHASE PRICE ALLOCATION OF ACQUISITION COSTS OF AN OPERATING PROPERTY

When an investor purchases a building, the purchase price of the transaction is presumed as an exchange for certain specific assets that are conveyed from the seller to the buyer. Accounting for acquisition of an operating real estate asset requires the allocation of the purchase price to these assets.

The purchase price paid by the buyer is allocated to these five items and recorded in the books of the buyer:

1. Land value

2. Building value as if vacant

3. Value of tenant relationships

4. Value of in-place leases

5. Value of above- and below-market leases

Land Value

The value of the land on which the building is built is normally obtained through appraisal of the land. The land value is separated from the total purchase price since land is usually not depreciated like other assets. In most property acquisitions, a cost segregation study is performed. The land value can be obtained from this study.

Building Value as if Vacant

In a purchase price allocation, the value of the building is determined without considering any lease present at the building. The value can be gotten from the appraisal report of the property obtained during due diligence. The building value would be recorded on the buyer's books under buildings and improvement and depreciated over its useful life.

Value of Tenant Relationships

A tenant relationship value exists where there are ongoing customer relationships in connection with current tenants that are of significant value to the building. An example of tenant relationship value includes major anchor tenants with a history of long-term leases at the building. Significant assumptions are required to determine this value; appraisers usually determine by amount. The values of tenant relationships are amortized over the remaining term of the tenants' leases on a straight-line basis.

Value of In-Place Leases

Leasing a space requires significant time and resources. A significant value difference exists between two identical properties where one property is leased to rent-paying tenants and the other is vacant. The building occupied by tenants will command significantly higher value compared to the vacant building for at least two main reasons: (1) It has current cash inflow and (2) no money is going to be spent to lease the building. An in-place lease is therefore the value of the tenant leases currently in the building. The value is determined based on the current and future rents as noted on the lease agreements. The values of in-place leases are amortized over the remaining term of the respective leases on a straight-line basis.

Value of Above- and Below-Market Leases

As noted, the value of leases currently in place at the building is determined based on the agreed rents of current and future tenants. Since these leases may have been in existence for some years at the time of the building's acquisition, when compared to current market rents, some of the in-place leases could either be higher or lower. Those leases with rents higher than current market leases are called above-market leases; those leases with rents lower than current market leases are called below-market leases. Above- and below-market lease values are recognized on the books of the buyer and amortized over the respective remaining lease terms on a straight-line basis. During purchase price allocation, above-market leases are recorded as assets; below-market leases are recorded as liabilities.

Allocation of the Asset's Values

After the determination of values for each of the assets and liabilities (land, building as if vacant, tenant relationships, in-place leases, above- and below-market leases), the total value is compared to the purchase price. There are two possible outcomes:

1. The total purchase price equals the total value determined. In this case, no adjustment is made on any of the component values determined.

2. The total purchase price is greater or less than the total value determined. This means the buyer paid more or less than the individual components of the acquired asset. The excess between the purchase price and the total value of the components should be allocated to each of the components based on their relative values. However, if the purchase price is lower than the value of the components, the values are reduced by this difference based also on their relative values.

It is important to note that the purchase price used in this allocation should not include acquisition costs incurred in acquiring the building, such as attorney's and broker's fees.

Example

A 200,000-square-foot building was acquired for $2,000,000. The values determined for each of the components acquired were:

Components	Values
Land	$ 600,000
Building as if vacant	$1,200,000
Tenant relationships	$ 150,000
In-place leases	$ 250,000
Above-market leases	$ 100,000
Below-market leases	$ (55,000)
Total	**$2,245,000**

The breakdown shows that the prices of the individual components of the assets acquired are higher than the purchase price paid by ($2,245,000 – $2,000,000) $245,000. This excess amount would be allocated among the various components as shown in Exhibit 13.1.

Exhibit 13.1   Allocation of Purchase Price Difference

	Initial Valuation	Pro Rated Value	Allocation of Difference	Purchase Price Allocation
Land	$ 600,000	27%	65,479	$ 534,521
Building as if vacant	$ 1,200,000	53%	130,958	$ 1,069,042
Tenant relationships	$ 150,000	7%	16,370	$ 133,630
In-place leases	$ 250,000	11%	27,283	$ 222,717
Above-market leases	$ 100,000	4%	10,913	$ 89,087
Below-market leases	$ (55,000)	–2%	(6,002)	$ (48,998)
Total value	$ 2,245,000	100%	245,000	$ 2,000,000
Purchase price	$ 2,000,000			
Difference	$ 245,000			

Based on the final allocated number from Exhibit 13.1, the initial purchase accounting journal entry that would be recorded would be:

Land	534,521	
Building and improvements	1,069,042	
In-place leases	133,630	
Tenant relationships	222,717	
Above-market leases	89,087	
Below-market leases		48,998
Cash		2,000,000
	2,048,998	2,048,998

(continued)

Monthly or quarterly amortization journal entries would be:

Depreciation Expense	xx	
Accumulated Depreciation		xx

(To record depreciation of building & improvements
over its useful life)

Amortization Expense	xx	
In-place lease—initial value		xx

(To record the amortization of the in-place leases over
the respective remaining lease terms)

Below-Market Leases	xx	
Rental Revenue		xx

(To record the amortization of below-market leases over
the respective remaining lease terms)

Rental Revenue	xx	
Above-Market Leases		xx

(To record the amortization of above-market leases over
the respective remaining lease terms)

14

ACCOUNTING FOR PROJECT DEVELOPMENT COSTS ON GAAP BASIS

STAGES OF REAL ESTATE DEVELOPMENT PROJECT

There are three main stages of a development project, and accounting at these stages can be different. The three main stages are:

1. Predevelopment stage

2. Development stage

3. Postdevelopment stage

Accounting for development projects under generally accepted accounting principles (GAAP) requires knowledge of regulatory requirements and pronouncements from various accounting bodies, such as the Financial Accounting Standards Board, American Institute of Certified Public Accountants (AICPA), Accounting Principles Board, and Emerging Issues Task Force, among others. The chapter aims to make these requirements and pronouncements simpler and easier to understand and also to offer a practical application of the pronouncements. This chapter also discusses the accounting for costs related to acquiring, developing, constructing, selling, and leasing real estate projects.

The costs associated with the development of a project are accounted in different ways, depending on the nature of the costs and the stage of the project. Some costs are expensed as period costs, some are capitalized when incurred as costs of the project, while others are recorded as prepaid expenses and expensed in the period in which the related revenues are recognized.

Predevelopment Stage

The predevelopment stage can be described as the period prior to the start of the construction of the project. Let us start the discussion of accounting for predevelopment from the very beginning, at the inception of the entity that will own the project. Normally the sponsor(s) of a project form a legal entity that directly owns the project (usually one of the limited liabilities entities discussed in Chapter 3). The start-up costs related to the formation of this legal entity should be expensed as incurred. These start-up costs include the related filing fees, legal fees, and other regulatory fees.

In the past, the accounting for start-up costs was handled differently by different companies in different industries. Some companies expensed their start-up costs while others capitalized them and amortized them over time. As a result of these inconsistencies, in April 1998 the AICPA Statement of Position No. 98-5, *Reporting on the Costs of Start-up Activities*, was issued.[1] It requires that start-up costs and organization costs are period costs and should be expensed instead of capitalized. This pronouncement was effective for financial statements for fiscal years beginning after December 15, 1998, although earlier adoption was encouraged; for certain entities that met the requirements for investment companies, their effective date was June 30, 1998.

Some examples of predevelopment costs related to a project itself include:

- Acquisition options
- Market studies
- Traffic studies
- Zoning changes
- Survey costs
- Costs of securing debt financing
- Costs of securing equity partners
- Marketing costs

---

1. American Institute of Certified Public Accountants, Statement of Position No. 98-5, *Reporting on the Costs of Start-up Activities* (1998).

It is important to pay particular attention to these costs to ensure that they are recorded correctly, as some are required to be expensed while others are required to be capitalized. GAAP requires that all costs associated with a project that are incurred prior to the acquisition of a property or before the entity obtains an option to acquire the property should be capitalized if all of these three conditions are met:

1. The costs are directly identifiable with the specific property.

2. The costs would be capitalized if the property were already acquired.

3. Acquisition of the property or of an option to acquire the property is probable.[2]

As mentioned, these three criteria have to be met for costs incurred prior to the acquisition of the property or option to acquire the property to be capitalized. The criteria require that such costs should be directly related to the property. Therefore, costs incurred at this stage should be examined carefully to make sure that they relate specifically to the property and are not general costs incurred by the entity. Some examples of directly related types of costs include project-related travel costs and consulting fees specifically related to the property prior to acquisition or obtaining option to acquire the property.

Another criterion mentioned is whether the cost would be capitalized had the property already been acquired. Therefore, the entity needs to assess whether the nature of the cost is such that it would be capitalized. An example is where the buyer, with the agreement of seller, decides to perform certain environmental tests prior to the decision on whether to purchase the property. Such costs clearly are costs a buyer would incur if the buyer already owned the property.

The last of the three criteria says that acquisition is probable. Here the test is both the ability of the buyer to close the deal and also that the subject property is available for sale. Therefore, even if the potential buyer is able and willing to purchase a particular property, if the property is not available for sale, this criterion is not met. Therefore, the costs should not be capitalized.

If the costs meet all three conditions mentioned, those costs are required to be capitalized; while all other costs should be expensed as incurred. It is also important to note that the cost to acquire an option to purchase a property must be capitalized. In most cases, even though all the criteria are met, there is no guarantee that the property would be acquired.

---

2. Financial Accounting Standards Board, FAS No. 67, Accounting for Costs and Initial Rental Operations of Real Estate Projects, paragraph 4 (2008).

Therefore, at any time when it becomes probable that the property would not be acquired, the prior capitalized costs would have to be expensed.

Other predevelopment costs that meet the criteria for capitalization include costs incurred to change the zoning of the site and costs incurred to obtain financing, such as loan fees, points, and origination fees. In most cases, the developer starts marketing the project prior to the start or completion of construction. Therefore, marketing and other selling costs would be incurred at different stages of development.

Development Stage

The development stage is the period with the most activities and costs among the three stages. It is also the longest period in the project development process. The accounting during this period is very important, as both a management and a cost control tool. Adequate care should be taken to ensure that costs are recorded in the correct cost category. Examples of costs incurred during this stage are:

- Site costs
- Architectural and engineering
- Financing
- Construction
- Taxes and insurance
- General and administrative
- Marketing
- Permits and licenses
- Contingencies

Normally in a construction project, a comprehensive budget is prepared with amounts for each of the cost categories just listed. The project's construction, management, accounting, and finance teams meet periodically to review the budget with the actual costs incurred to ensure that costs incurred are recorded in the correct cost category or trade and also that the budget and amount left to complete the project are still reasonable.

A typical construction cost summary report with the related budget and actual costs is shown in Exhibit 14.1.

As in other stages of the development process, some costs incurred during the development stage are capitalized while some are expensed based on the GAAP rules. According to Statement of Financial Accounting Standards No. 67, paragraph 7: "Project costs clearly associated with the acquisition, development, and construction of a real estate project shall be

Exhibit 14.1 Construction Cost Summary

Cost Components	Project Current Cost	Draw 1	Draw 2	Draw 3	Draw 4	Draw 5	Draw 6	Total Actual	Cost to Complete
Site Costs									
Site Costs	3,200,000	3,200,000	—	—	—	—	—	3,200,000	—
Subtotal Site Costs	**3,200,000**	**3,200,000**	**—**	**—**	**—**	**—**	**—**	**3,200,000**	**—**
Architectural/Engineering									
Design Architect	450,000	50,000	40,000	75,000	43,000	57,000	10,000	275,000	175,000
Production Architect	260,000	20,000	10,000	16,000	—	12,000	5,000	63,000	197,000
Interior Design	100,000	—	2,000	4,000	—	—	—	6,000	94,000
Residential Interior Design	100,000	—	3,000	5,000	—	—	—	8,000	92,000
Landscape Architect	20,000	—	—	1,000	—	—	—	1,000	19,000
Structural Engineer	90,000	10,000	13,000	30,000	26,000	—	—	79,000	11,000
Mechanical Engineer	120,000	—	25,000	30,000	10,000	—	—	65,000	55,000
Security/Teledata Systems	10,000	—	—	—	—	—	—	—	10,000
Surveying	25,000	10,000	10,000	—	—	—	—	20,000	5,000
Civil Engineering	25,000	10,000	5,000	—	—	—	—	15,000	10,000
Controlled Inspections	50,000	5,000	15,000	—	—	—	—	20,000	30,000
Subtotal Architectural	**1,250,000**	**105,000**	**123,000**	**161,000**	**79,000**	**69,000**	**15,000**	**552,000**	**698,000**
Construction									
Base Building General Conditions	18,500,000	500,000	100,000	200,000	250,000	158,000	100,000	1,308,000	17,192,000
Consultant	50,000	2,000	5,000	2,000	1,000	5,000	8,000	23,000	27,000
Subtotal Construction	**18,550,000**	**502,000**	**105,000**	**202,000**	**251,000**	**163,000**	**108,000**	**1,331,000**	**17,219,000**
Taxes									
Taxes	350,000	—	—	—	—	—	—	—	350,000
Subtotal Taxes	**350,000**	**—**	**—**	**—**	**—**	**—**	**—**	**—**	**350,000**
Insurance									
Insurance	150,000	5,000	5,000	5,000	5,000	5,000	5,000	30,000	120,000
Subtotal Insurance	**150,000**	**5,000**	**5,000**	**5,000**	**5,000**	**5,000**	**5,000**	**30,000**	**120,000**

(continued)

Exhibit 14.1 (Continued)

Cost Components	Project Current Cost	Draw 1	Draw 2	Draw 3	Draw 4	Draw 5	Draw 6	Total Actual	Cost to Complete
Financing									
Loan interests	2,000,000	50,000	50,000	50,000	50,000	50,000	50,000	300,000	1,700,000
Financing Cost	300,000	—	300,000	—	—	—	—	300,000	—
Subtotal Financing Cost	**2,300,000**	**50,000**	**350,000**	**50,000**	**50,000**	**50,000**	**50,000**	**600,000**	**1,700,000**
Leasing									
Retail Commissions	65,000	—	—	—	—	—	—	—	65,000
Residential Sales Commissions	500,000	—	—	—	—	—	—	—	500,000
Residential Marketing	100,000	—	—	—	—	—	10,000	10,000	90,000
Retail Space Planning	25,000	10,000	5,000	—	—	—	—	15,000	10,000
Legal Leasing	50,000	—	—	—	—	—	—	—	50,000
Sales Center	200,000	—	—	50,000	5,000	5,000	5,000	65,000	135,000
Marketing Consulting	15,000	—	—	—	—	1,000	2,000	3,000	12,000
Building Model	95,000	10,000	2,000	20,000	10,000	—	—	42,000	53,000
Collateral Materials	20,000	—	—	5,000	5,000	—	—	10,000	10,000
Advertising/Mailing	25,000	—	—	—	—	5,000	2,500	7,500	17,500
Public Relations Fees	60,000	10,000	5,000	—	—	5,000	2,000	22,000	38,000
Website/Sales Operations	25,000	—	15,000	5,000	—	—	—	20,000	5,000
Subtotal Leasing	**1,180,000**	**30,000**	**27,000**	**80,000**	**20,000**	**16,000**	**21,500**	**194,500**	**985,500**
General & Administrative									
General & Administrative	200,000	5,000	5,000	5,000	5,000	5,000	5,000	30,000	170,000
Subtotal General & Administrative	**200,000**	**5,000**	**5,000**	**5,000**	**5,000**	**5,000**	**5,000**	**30,000**	**170,000**
Contingency									
Contingency	1,000,000	—	—	—	—	—	—	—	1,000,000
Subtotal Contingency	**1,000,000**	—	—	—	—	—	—	—	**1,000,000**
TOTAL BUDGET	**28,180,000**	**3,897,000**	**615,000**	**503,000**	**410,000**	**308,000**	**204,500**	**5,937,500**	**22,242,500**

capitalized as a cost of that project."[3] The implication here is that for a cost to be capitalized as a project cost, there has to be a clear indication that it is directly related to a project. Many costs incurred at this stage are mostly capitalized, such as site acquisition costs, architectural, engineering, and construction. However, certain other costs incurred during this stage that are not directly associated with the project should be expensed; these costs include general and administrative and marketing costs. The invoices and other supporting documents related to these costs should be properly reviewed to determine the nature of the costs and to decide whether they should be capitalized or expensed.

In some instances, costs might be related to more than one project. For example, say a developer is developing an office complex with multiple individual buildings, and bills for certain costs, such as surveys or architects for the whole complex, are billed together. Such costs are still capitalized, but they would have to be allocated among the individual buildings. The developer should use any reasonable method to allocate the costs among the individual projects.

Amortization of Costs   Financing costs such as origination fees, points, and guaranty fees should be capitalized as prepaid assets and amortized to periodic project costs.

Example

Assume an entity obtained a construction loan of $100 million for an office development project due at the completion of the project in 3 years with an interest rate of 8 percent. At closing, the borrower paid 1 percent origination fee, 1 percent point, .05 percent debt guaranty fee, and other loan closing costs of $525,000.

Therefore, the total costs incurred by the borrower at closing, which are usually disbursed from the loan principal, would be:

Origination fee (1%)	$1,000,000
Point (1%)	1,000,000
Guaranty fee (.05%)	500,000
Other loan closing costs	525,000
Total loan closing costs	$3,025,000

At the day of closing, the entity would record this accounting journal entry:

Cash	$96,975,000	
Prepaid assets	3,025,000	
Loans payable		$100,000,000

---

3. Financial Accounting Standards Board (2008).

Note, however, that in most cases the borrower would not take the cash up front at closing but will draw on the amount periodically (usually once a month) as bills are received from contractors and vendors through a process called the submission of draw.

On the amortization of the $3,025,000 total loan closing costs, each month the company reduces the prepaid asset by $84,028 ($3,025,000/ 36 months). Therefore, each month, the journal entry to record this amount as project cost would be:

Loan financing cost	$84,028	
Prepaid assets—loan cost		$84,028

This entry will be recorded each month over the 36-month loan term. If for any reason the loan term is extended, the monthly amortization will have to be adjusted.

Example

Assume that six months prior to the loan expiration, the company realized that the project would not be timely completed due to a construction workers' union strike. Management assessment indicates that the project will take an additional six months from the prior expected completion date. The borrower therefore approaches the lender, which agrees to extend the loan for the additional six months. The unamortized prepaid balance would now be amortized over the remaining loan term of one year, which is determined as the six months left on the original agreement plus the additional six-month extension.

The new monthly amortization would be determined as:

Unamortized balance prior to loan extension ($84,028 × 6)	= $504,167
New amortization period	= 12 months
Monthly amortization ($504,167/12 months)	= $42,014

Therefore, after the extension, the monthly journal entry to record the cost amortization would be:

Loan financing cost	$42,014	
Prepaid asset—loan cost		$42,014

Real Estate and Income Taxes   During construction, the entity may be required to pay taxes to the government. The most common taxes are the real estate taxes and income taxes. These two taxes are treated very differently in a construction project. For GAAP financial reporting purposes, costs incurred for real estate taxes from the inception of the project through the time at which the property is ready for its intended use should be capitalized as project costs. Real estate taxes after this period should be expensed. (See the detailed discussion in the "Postdevelopment Stage" section.)

The second type of taxes mentioned was income taxes. During the development stage, companies can still earn income through interest income on funds deposited at a bank or through parking revenues. Therefore, an entity might owe the government income taxes related to this income. These income taxes are expenses of the period and should be expensed.

Often some companies net their interest expense against interest income on their project budget; however, financial reporting under GAAP does not allow the netting of these two costs in financial statements. As mentioned earlier, interest expense incurred through the time at which the property is ready for its intended use should be capitalized; interest income should be reported separately on the income statement when earned. The only exception in which interest income can be netted against interest expense is when the interest expense is from tax-exempt borrowings. Another common error in financial reporting by some entities is the accounting for audit fees paid to the entity's auditors for the audit of its financial statements. Audit fees are expenses of the period and not directly related to the project. Therefore, they should be expensed as incurred. In general, all expenses should be thoroughly reviewed to determine whether they should be expensed or capitalized.

POSTDEVELOPMENT STAGE

The postdevelopment stage is the period when the project is substantially complete and is ready for its intended use. For example, if this is a condo project, the buyers can now move in; if it is a rental property, the lessees, if any, can now take possession of the spaces.

Most expenses incurred during this stage, such as salaries and wages, cleaning, security, utilities, water, and real estate taxes, are expensed as incurred. In addition, certain capital improvements performed after the completion of the project normally are capitalized and depreciated over the project's useful life. Also, certain costs incurred in leasing the space (if a rental property), such as brokers' fees and attorney's fees, are also capitalized and amortized over the related lease term.

15

DEVELOPMENT PROJECT REVENUE RECOGNITIONS

The process and methodology of revenue recognition depend on the type of project. The revenue recognition for sale of condominium units is very different from that for the sale of an office building or apartment building after they are built. It is also different from the revenue recognition of the rental of any office or apartment building. This chapter discusses these types of projects and the revenue recognition methods.

Examples of rental properties include office space, residential apartments, retail shopping centers, warehouses, and hotels. Revenues from the rental of spaces from these types of properties are not recognized until the projects are substantially completed and held available for occupancy. A project is defined as substantially complete and held available for occupancy when the developer has completed tenant improvements but no longer than one year after major construction activity has been completed.

Generally accepted accounting principles (GAAP) require that revenue should be recognized when earned. The revenue from a month-to-month rental of a space is recognized when the rent is due from the tenant. However, for long-term leases (leases for periods over one year), GAAP requires that the revenue should be recognized on a straight-line basis unless another systematic and rational basis is more representative of the beneficial usage of the leased property. See Chapter 4 for a detailed description of this revenue recognition method.

The profits and revenues from the sale of real estate are accounted for in various ways, depending on the nature of transaction. The six most common methods of profit recognition are:

1. Full accrual method
2. Deposit method

3. Installment method

4. Reduced-profit method

5. Percentage-of-completion method

6. Cost recovery method

FULL ACCRUAL METHOD

The full accrual method is one of the methods of real estate profit recognition in which the full sale price and profits are recognized when the real estate is sold. For the full accrual method to be used, the transaction has to meet two main conditions:

1. The profit can be reasonably determined.

2. The seller's obligation to the buyer is complete.

The profit from the sales transaction can be reasonably determined if there is reasonable assurance that the sales price of the transaction is collectible from the buyer and any portion of the sale price that is not collectible can be reasonably estimated.

Example 1

Citi Development Corp., a developer of office properties, sold a recently completed 150,000 square-foot office property in Greenwich, Connecticut, to Enrone Corp. for $95 million. When the parties signed the commitment agreement for the transaction, Enrone paid $40 million and an additional $40 million at closing 3 months later. Enrone agreed to pay the remaining $15 million over 15 months with principal and interest due monthly. At closing Citi Development has no remaining obligation to Enrone and therefore can recognize the full profit from the sale. In this example both conditions were met; therefore the full accrual method should be used.

Example 2

Assume in the Citi Development example, that while the property is still under construction Enrone pays the full contract amount of $95 million. In this case, the developer still has remaining obligation of completing construction of the property. Therefore, the full accrual method cannot be used in recognizing any profit from the payment received from Enrone.

If the two criteria are not met, the seller has to determine which other methods would be appropriate. However, in addition to the two main conditions noted above, a transaction has to meet these four additional criteria:

1. A final sale between the buyer and the seller has been consummated such that all the obligations between the parties have been fulfilled and all conditions prior to closing have been met.

2. The buyer has sufficient initial and continuing investment in the transaction to demonstrate its ability and willingness to fulfill its obligation. This ensures that the buyer has enough skin in the deal to avoid backing out of the transaction. The buyer can meet this requirement by providing enough down payments, an irrevocable letter of credit from an independent financially viable lending institution, or full payment of the asset's purchase price.

3. In cases where the buyer did not pay for the purchase price in full at the time of closing, the remaining amount due to the seller is not subject to any future subordination after the sale. This also means that in the event of default by the buyer, none of the buyer's debt obligations would have preferential claim on the property higher than the seller's claim on the property.

4. The sale transfers all the rights, risks, and rewards of ownership of the property to the buyer. The seller should not have any substantial remaining obligation to the buyer in relation to the sale. An example would be a development project where the completion and delivery date is still in the future. In this case, the seller still has substantial remaining obligation to deliver a completed premises to the buyer at a future date. Thus, the full accrual method would not be used in recognizing the total profit.

If it is determined that the transaction meets the criteria for full accrual method, the entry to record the transaction by the seller (e.g., the sale of a property for $20 million) would be:

Cash	$20,000,000	
Sales		$20,000,000

Initial Investment   Criterion 2 above requires that buyer has sufficient initial investment in the transaction, so for the buyer's initial investments requirement to be met, GAAP provides that the initial investment shall be equal to at least a major part of the difference between usual loan limits for that type of property in that market and the sales value of the property. Exhibit 15.1 provides a guide to determine the adequacy of the initial investment, which in most cases represents the buyer's down payment.

Exhibit 15.1 Minimum Initial Investment

Type of Property	Minimum Initial Investment Expressed as a Percentage of Sales Value
Land:	
Held for commercial, industrial, or residential development to commence within two years after sale	20
Held for commercial, industrial, or residential development to commence after two years	25
Commercial and Industrial Property:	
Office and industrial buildings, shopping centers, etc.:	
Properties subject to lease on a long-term lease basis to parties with satisfactory credit rating; cash flow currently sufficient to service all indebtedness	10
Single-tenancy properties sold to a buyer with a satisfactory credit rating	15
All other	20
Other income-producing properties (hotels, motels, marinas, mobile home parks, etc.):	
Cash flow currently sufficient to service all indebtedness	15
Start-up situation or current deficiencies in cash flow	25
Multifamily Residential Property:	
Primary residence:	
Cash flow currently sufficient to service all indebtedness	10
Start-up situations or current deficiencies in cash flow	15
Secondary or recreational residence:	
Cash flow currently sufficient to service all indebtedness	15
Start-up situations or current deficiencies in cash flow	25
Single-Family Residential Property (including condominium or cooperative housing):	
Primary residence of the buyer	5
Secondary or recreational residence	10

Source: Financial Accounting Standards Board, FAS No. 66, paragraph 54, Accounting for Sales of Real Estate (October 1982).

GAAP also requires that for recently obtained permanent loan or firm permanent loan commitment for maximum financing of the property, the minimum initial investment by the buyer should be whichever of the following is greater:

    a. The minimum percentage of the sales value . . . of the property as noted [in Exhibit 15.1].

b. The lesser of:

1. The amount of the sales value of the property in excess of 115 percent of the amount of a newly placed permanent loan or firm permanent loan commitment from a primary lender that is an independent established lending institution.

2. Twenty-five percent of the sales value.[1]

Example

A condominium unit purchased as the buyer's secondary residence is sold for $1 million, and the buyer provided an initial deposit of $150,000. Assume in this example that the loan for the remaining balance of $850,000 was from an independent established lending institution.

    To determine if the $150,000 initial deposit is sufficient to establish the buyer's commitment using the minimum initial investment criteria, this analysis should be performed.

Analysis:

(a)	Minimum percentage of the sales value per Minimum Initial Investment Table (10%)	$100,000
(b)(1)	Sales value in excess 115% of loan ($1,000,000 – ($850,000 × 115%)	$22,500
(2)	25% of the sales value ($1,000,000 × 25%)	$250,000

    In this analysis, the required minimum initial investment should be $100,000. This amount is determined by first calculating (a), then obtaining the lesser of (b)(1) ($22,500) or (b)(2) ($250,000). The minimum initial investment is the greater of (a) ($100,000) and (b) ($22,500).

    It is important to note that the initial deposit used in the analysis of minimum initial investment is the nonrefundable part of the deposit if the agreement has a refundable deposit clause.

Continuing Investment   In addition, criterion 2 for use of full accrual method requires that the buyer has sufficient continuing investment in the transaction. Continuing investment relates to the buyer's payment of the remaining purchase price after the initial investment in the transaction. The Statement of Financial Accounting Standards No. 66, paragraph 12, says:

---

1. FAS 66, paragraph 53, Accounting for Sales of Real Estate (October 1982).

The buyer's continuing investment in a real estate transaction shall not qualify unless the buyer is contractually required to pay each year on its total debt for the purchase price of the property an amount at least equal to the level annual payment that would be needed to pay that debt and interest on the unpaid balance over no more than (a) 20 years for debt for land and (b) the customary amortization term of a first mortgage loan by an independent established lending institution for other real estate.[2]

In other words, after the buyer makes the initial investment in a real estate purchase, the remaining amount due to the seller, which in most cases is financed through an independent lender, should at a minimum have financing terms as mentioned. This criterion is viewed as an indication of the buyer's ability to acquire the assets and also fulfills the borrower's obligations on the transaction.

DEPOSIT METHOD

The deposit method is one of the methods that can be used when a real estate transaction does not meet the conditions and criteria required for the full accrual of profits. Under this method, no profit, receivables, or sales are recognized; however, the seller can disclose in its financial statements that the asset is subject to a sales contract.

This method is used to record the initial and continuing investments in a real estate transaction made by the buyer prior to consummation of sales. The deposit method is also the appropriate method of accounting for a transaction where the recovery of the project's cost, in the event of the buyer's default, is not assured. Examples of real estate transactions where the deposit method may be used are:

- The sale has not yet been consummated; thus the deal has not yet closed, or there are remaining obligations between the parties required before consummation that have not been fulfilled.

- The buyer meets all the criteria for the full accrual method except that the initial investment and the recovery of the project's cost cannot be assured if the buyer defaults.

- Condominium projects where one or more of the four criteria required for the percentage-of-completion method (PCM) has not been met. (See the discussion on the "Percentage-of-Completion Method.")

---

2. Financial Accounting Standards Boards, Accounting for Sales of Real Estate (1982).

- A real estate transaction where the seller guarantees a return on the investment for a limited period of time. The agreed-upon costs and expenses incurred prior to the operation of the property should be accounted for using the deposit method. However, if the guarantee is for an extended period, the transaction should be accounted for as a financing, leasing, or profit-sharing arrangement, depending on other specific terms of the transaction.

Example

Patterson Construction Corp., a developer of industrial warehouse and manufacturing facilities, is developing an industrial park built-to-suit. A start-up plastics manufacturer signs a contract to purchase one of the 20 warehouse units at the park at a purchase price of $1.7 million. Prior to the signing of the sale agreement, the buyer provided the seller deposit money representing 10 percent of purchase price. Assume that the sale has not been consummated and the seller has determined that in an event of default by the buyer, the cost of the property would not be recovered due to reasons such as property location or design uniqueness. In this type of situation, when the seller collects the 10 percent deposit, the amount should be recorded by the developer as a deposit with this journal entry:

Cash	$170,000	
Buyer deposit liability		$170,000

Any subsequent continuing investments by the buyer would be recorded with similar entries as above until sale is consummated and the ownership rights, rewards, and obligations pass to the buyer.

At closing, when all the conditions required for consummation of sale and full accrual are met, the seller would then recognize the sale with this journal entry:

Deposit liability	$1,700,000	
Sales		$1,700,000

This entry reduces to zero the liability that has been recognized from the prior deposits received by the seller and also recognizes the sale as a result of the transfer of the risks and rewards of the asset from the seller to the buyer.

In this exercise we focus on the revenue-related journal entries. Note, however, that other journal entries would have to be recorded to recognize the related cost of sales, which prior to now were being capitalized as work in progress (WIP).

Assume that the total cost of the unit sold to the plastics company was $1 million. This amount, which was recorded when incurred as WIP, will be recognized in the income statement as cost of sales with this entry:

Cost of sales	$1,000,000	
Work in progress		$1,000,000

This entry should be recorded at the same time as the total sales is recognized. In essence, it matches the cost of sales with the related sales recognized.

INSTALLMENT METHOD

The installment method is the appropriate method where both:

1. A transaction would have qualified under the full accrual method except that the buyer's initial minimum criteria were not met; and

2. The cost of the property could be recovered by reselling the property in the event the buyer is not able to fulfill its obligation under the terms of the agreement.

Under the installment method, each payment made by the buyer to the seller is allocated between cost and profit using the same ratio by which total cost of the project and total project profit is proportional to the sales price.

Example

ABC Corp. sells a property to DMV Corp. for $2 million. DMV paid a cash down payment of $100,000 with the remaining balance financed by ABC Corp. For purposes of this exercise, it is assumed that the buyer's initial investment did not meet the initial minimum criteria and therefore will be accounted for using the installment method.

Based on the above information:

Total sales price	= $2,000,000
Total cost	= $1,200,000
Total profit	= $ 800,000
Profit % = 800,000/2,000,000 = 40%	

At the time the sale was consummated, ABC will record the sales, the gross profit that was deferred, and the total cost of the sale with this entry:

(i)	Cash	$100,000	
	Accounts receivable		1,100,000
	Sales		$1,200,000

(To recognize sales, cash receipt, and receivables)

(ii)	Cost of sales	$1,200,000	
	Real Estate Property		$1,200,000

(To recognize related cost of sales and remove assets from books)

(iii)	Deferred sales profit	$440,000	
	Deferred assets from uncollected receivables		$440,000

(To recognize deferred receivables; amount is determined as: 40% × $1,100,000 = $440,000)

As more of the receivables are collected from the buyer, the seller will recognize the deferred profit from the sale. Assume that the next month DMV remitted the contracted monthly payment of $50,000; the entry to recognize this receivable and the related deferred profit would be:

(i)	Cash	$50,000	
	Receivables		$50,000

(To record the receipt of the receivables)

(ii)	Deferred assets from uncollected receivables		$20,000
	Profit recognized	$20,000	

(To recognized the prior deferred profit; 40% × $50,000 = $20,000)

The income statement of ABC Corp. immediately after this transaction would look like this:

ABC CORP.
INCOME STATEMENT

Revenues:	
Sales	$ 2,000,000
Deferred profit	(440,000)
	$ 1,560,000
Costs:	
Cost of sales	1,200,000
	1,200,000
Net income	$ 360,000

REDUCED-PROFIT METHOD

In the discussion on the installment method, we mentioned situations where a transaction meets all the criteria for full profit accrual except that the initial investment criteria were not met. The reduced-profit method is similar to the installment method. The reduced-profit method of profit recognition is used where all the criteria of full profit recognition are met *except* that the continuing investment criteria were not met. However, for profit to be re-corded using this method, the annual payments by the buyer should at least equal:

1. The interest and principal amortization on the maximum first mort-gage debt that could be used to finance the property; plus

2. Interest on the difference between the total actual debt on the property and the maximum first mortgage debt.

Remember, the criterion to meet "continuing investment" is that the buyer is contractually required under the debt agreement of the total debt on the property to pay each year an amount equal to at least principal and interest payment over the customary amortization term of a first mortgage loan by an independent reputable lending institution. For a land purchase, the appropriate payment period is determined to be 20 years.

Example

An office property located in downtown Houston, Texas, with cost to seller of $15 million was sold for $20 million. The buyer paid a down payment of $3 million and obtained a $14 million first mortgage from an independent lending institution at a rate of 10 percent over 20 years. In addition, the seller provided a second mortgage financing to the buyer of additional $3 million with interest of 8 percent over 25 years. The interest on both loans is com-pounded monthly.

Assume that the down payment of $3 million is the minimum initial in-vestment requirement and that the customary first-mortgage financing for this type of property in this market would be over 20 years with a market rate of 11 percent.

On this transaction, since the second-mortgage financing by the seller is for 25 years (which is above the term to meet the continuing investment crite-ria for this type of property), the total profit of $5 million that should have been recognized at the time of the sale is reduced, and the deferred profit is recognized from years 21 through 25.

The calculation is determined as:

Total sales price	$ 20,000,000
Total cost to seller	$ 15,000,000
Total Profit	$ 5,000,000

As mentioned, the total sales price is comprised of:

Buyer's deposit	$ 3,000,000
First mortgage from independent lender	$ 14,000,000
Second mortgage from seller	$ 3,000,000
Total sales price	$ 20,000,000

The buyer's monthly payment based on the terms of the debt agreement on the $3 million second mortgage is calculated as:

Loan amount	$3,000,000
Term in months (25 yrs × 12)	300
Rate	8%
Monthly payment	$23,001

Therefore, the present value of the $23,001 monthly payment for 20 years would be:

Monthly payment	$ 23,001
Market rate	11%
Customary market term in months (20 yrs × 12)	240
Present value	$ 2,248,799
Deferred profit ($3,000,000 – $2,248,799)	$ 751,201

The profit recognized at the time of sale would be:

Sales price	$ 20,000,000
Cost	$ 15,000,000
Deferred profit	$ 751,201
Profit recognized at time of sale	$ 4,248,799

So, in years 21 through 25, the deferred profit of $751,201 would be recognized as the mortgage payments are recovered. The straight-line method (or another reasonable method) can be used in recognizing this deferred profit from years 21 through 25.

PERCENTAGE-OF-COMPLETION METHOD

The percentage-of-completion method is a revenue recognition methodology in which revenues and profits are recognized as construction progresses if certain specific criteria are met. This method is used mostly in condominium and time-sharing projects, where the units are sold individually.

For a project to be recorded using the percentage-of-completion method, five criteria must be met:

1. The construction project has passed the preliminary stage.

The preliminary stage of a project has not been completed if certain elements of the project have not be completed, such as surveys, project design, execution of construction and architectural contracts, site preparation and clearance, excavation, completion of foundation work, and similar aspects of the project. These criteria are some of the basic requirements before a percentage-of-completion method can be used in accounting for a condominium or time-sharing project.

2. GAAP requires that the "buyer is committed to the extent of being unable to require a refund except for non-delivery of the unit or interest."[3]

The determination of whether the buyer is committed to buy the unit or interest requires judgment; however, one way to make this determination is to utilize the minimum initial investment criteria. It is important to understand that the purpose of determining the buyer's commitment is to ensure that the buyer has more skin in the transaction and prevent the buyer from easily walking away at any slight change in the market.

The minimum initial investment requirement provides a guide that can be used to determine the buyer's commitment in the transaction and is shown in Figure 15.1. The percentages listed are based on usual loan limits for different types of properties.

3. The project should have sufficient units sold to ensure that the project will not regress to rental.

Obviously, the percentage-of-completion method is used to recognize revenue and profit while the project is still ongoing based on the assumption that the units will be completed and sold to buyers, not rented to tenants. This criterion ensures that the objective is achieved. To prevent the possibility that the developer, after recognizing some revenues and profits related to the units sold, then reverts the project to a rental property, the developer is required to sell sufficient units before using the percentage-of-completion method. The determination of how many units are sufficient requires significant judgment, but the decision must be made based on the nature of the project, the market for that particular type of project, and the local and regional economy where the project is located.

4. The agreed-on sales price of the units of interest should be determinable and collectible.

The collection of the sales price can be assumed to be assured if the buyer meets the initial investment and continuing investment criteria discussed earlier under the "Full Accrual Method." It could be difficult to establish that the sales price is collectible if the buyer is unable to meet those criteria.

5. The total aggregate sales amounts and costs for all the units can be reasonably determined.

---

3. Ibid., paragraph 37.

Because the determination of the periodic profits to be recognized is based on the estimated aggregate sales proceeds and estimated total cost of the project, it is crucial that these two numbers can be reasonably estimated. If these numbers cannot be estimated, the percentage-of-completion method is not allowed.

Any condominium or time-share project that does not meet any of these criteria can record the deposits received from the buyer using the deposit method.

Example

Hill Corp. Inc. is developing a 30-unit condominium project in Washington, DC, with retail and parking components. The condominium portion is approximately 60,000 square feet; the retail and parking portions are 10,000 and 6,000 square feet, respectively. The condominium units are expected to sell for $2,000 per square foot with estimated cost of $1,100 per square foot. The retail and parking sections would not be sold but would be rented to tenants upon completion. The retail and parking sections are estimated to cost $600 and $400 per square foot, respectively.

A breakdown of the 30 condominium units is:

Unit No.	No. Bedrooms	Size	Estimated Cost	Expected Sales Price
1	2	1,600	$ 1,760,000	$ 3,200,000
2	2	1,600	$ 1,760,000	$ 3,200,000
3	2	1,600	$ 1,760,000	$ 3,200,000
4	1	1,300	$ 1,430,000	$ 2,600,000
5	3	2,300	$ 2,530,000	$ 4,600,000
6	3	2,300	$ 2,530,000	$ 4,600,000
7	4	2,800	$ 3,080,000	$ 5,600,000
8	2	1,600	$ 1,760,000	$ 3,200,000
9	2	1,600	$ 1,760,000	$ 3,200,000
10	1	1,300	$ 1,430,000	$ 2,600,000
11	1	1,300	$ 1,430,000	$ 2,600,000
12	1	1,300	$ 1,430,000	$ 2,600,000
13	4	2,800	$ 3,080,000	$ 5,600,000
14	4	2,800	$ 3,080,000	$ 5,600,000
15	2	1,600	$ 1,760,000	$ 3,200,000
16	2	1,600	$ 1,760,000	$ 3,200,000
17	4	2,800	$ 3,080,000	$ 5,600,000
18	3	2,300	$ 2,530,000	$ 4,600,000
19	3	2,300	$ 2,530,000	$ 4,600,000
20	2	1,600	$ 1,760,000	$ 3,200,000
21	4	2,800	$ 3,080,000	$ 5,600,000

(*continued*)

(*continued*)				
22	4	2,800	$ 3,080,000	$ 5,600,000
23	2	1,600	$ 1,760,000	$ 3,200,000
24	3	2,300	$ 2,530,000	$ 4,600,000
25	3	2,300	$ 2,530,000	$ 4,600,000
26	2	1,600	$ 1,760,000	$ 3,200,000
27	2	1,600	$ 1,760,000	$ 3,200,000
28	1	1,300	$ 1,430,000	$ 2,600,000
29	3	2,300	$ 2,530,000	$ 4,600,000
30	4	3,000	$ 3,300,000	$ 6,000,000
		60,000	$66,000,000	$120,000,000

Exhibit 15.2 presents the budget prepared for this development project. Note that the budget categories can be further detailed for better analysis of the costs.

Exhibit 15.2   Sample Development Project Budget

Cost Categories	Parking	Retail	Condominium	Total
Site Costs	1,184,211	1,973,684	11,842,105	15,000,000
Architectual/Engineering:				
Interior Design	—	—	450,000	450,000
Design Architect	39,474	65,789	394,737	500,000
Production Architect	23,684	39,474	236,842	300,000
Surveying	5,921	9,868	59,211	75,000
Residential Interior Design	15,789	26,316	157,895	200,000
Landscape Architect	11,842	19,737	118,421	150,000
Civil Engineering	27,632	46,053	276,316	350,000
Structural Engineer	27,632	46,053	276,316	350,000
Mechanical Engineer	27,632	46,053	276,316	350,000
Security/Teledata Systems	27,632	46,053	276,316	350,000
Geotechnical Engineer	13,816	23,026	138,158	175,000
Subtotal Architectural/Engineering	**221,053**	**368,421**	**2,660,526**	**3,250,000**
Construction:				
Excavation/Foundation	347,368	578,947	3,473,684	4,400,000
Hollow Metal/Hardware	181,579	302,632	1,815,789	2,300,000
Roll Down Gate	1,579	2,632	15,789	20,000
Skylights	—	—	350,000	350,000
Curtainwall	—	—	4,500,000	4,500,000
Drywall	276,316	460,526	2,763,158	3,500,000
Tile/Stone	161,842	269,737	1,618,421	2,050,000
Wood Flooring	—	10,000	1,490,000	1,500,000
Carpet	—	—	750,000	750,000
Painting	94,737	157,895	947,368	1,200,000
Fire Extinguishers	5,921	9,868	59,211	75,000

Toilet Accessories	35,526	59,211	355,263	450,000
Window Washing Equip.	—	33,553	221,447	255,000
Appliances	197,368	328,947	1,973,684	2,500,000
Kitchen Cabinets	—	—	2,600,000	2,600,000
Window Treatments	—	—	200,000	200,000
Pools	—	—	1,850,000	1,850,000
Elevators	—	—	2,650,000	2,650,000
Plumbing	276,316	460,526	2,763,158	3,500,000
HVAC	197,368	328,947	1,973,684	2,500,000
Electrical	276,316	460,526	2,763,158	3,500,000
Subtotal Construction	**2,052,237**	**3,463,947**	**35,133,816**	**40,650,000**
Capitalized Taxes and Insurance:				
Real Estate Taxes	146,053	243,421	1,460,526	1,850,000
Insurance	23,684	39,474	236,842	300,000
Subtotal Capitalized Taxes and Insurance	**169,737**	**282,895**	**1,697,368**	**2,150,000**
Financing:				
Interest Cost	252,632	421,053	2,526,316	3,200,000
Loan Closing Costs	51,316	85,526	513,158	650,000
Subtotal Financing	**303,947**	**506,579**	**3,039,474**	**3,850,000**
Capitalized Leasing:				
Retail Space Planning	150,000	—	—	150,000
Sales Center	—	—	200,000	200,000
Building Model	—	—	318,816	318,816
Creative Direction	11,842	19,737	118,421	150,000
Collateral Materials	6,711	11,184	67,105	85,000
Subtotal Leasing	**168,553**	**30,921**	**704,342**	**903,816**
Capitalized General & Administrative	**513,158**	**855,263**	**5,131,579**	**6,500,000**
Contingency	**631,579**	**1,052,632**	**6,315,789**	**8,000,000**
SUBTOTAL BUDGETED—Capitalized Costs	**5,244,474**	**8,534,342**	**66,525,000**	**80,303,816**
Marketing—Expensed Component				
Retail Commissions	—	800,000	—	800,000
Condominium Closing Costs	—	—	1,000,000	1,000,000
Residential Marketing	—	—	250,000	250,000
Marketing Consulting Fees	—	—	120,000	120,000
Public Relations	—	—	100,000	100,000
Creative Direction	3,947	6,579	39,474	50,000
Subtotal Marketing—Expensed Component	**3,947**	**806,579**	**1,509,474**	**2,320,000**
Expensed General & Administrative	**9,474**	**15,789**	**94,737**	**120,000**
Income Taxes	—	—	**169,806**	**169,806**
Misc Income	**(229,902)**	**(383,169)**	**(2,299,017)**	**(2,912,088)**
TOTAL PROJECT BUDGET	**5,027,993**	**8,973,541**	**66,000,000**	**80,001,534**

In addition, care must be taken to ensure that costs are appropriately classified between capitalized and expensed costs. Expensed costs are period costs that are recognized on the income statement. Capitalized costs become cost of sales when the related revenues are recognized. Note also that certain costs are recorded as prepaid assets and later are recognized as costs when certain events take place. An example is prepayment for marketing of the condo units.

In this example, it is assumed that the capitalized costs would be a good measure of the project's percentage of completion. Let us also assume that after one year since the start of construction, the actual capitalized costs incurred in the project are $27,030,000, which is allocated as shown:

Condominium	$21,355,263
Retail	3,484,211
Parking	2,190,526

Exhibit 15.3 shows a detailed breakout of these costs among condominium, retail, and parking portions.

Exhibit 15.3   Actual Project Cost Incurred after One Year

Cost Categories	Parking	Retail	Condominium	Total
Site Costs	1,184,211	1,973,684	11,842,105	15,000,000
Architectual/Engineering:				
Interior Design	—	—	—	—
Design Architect	5,921	9,868	59,211	75,000
Production Architect	3,553	5,921	35,526	45,000
Surveying	5,921	9,868	59,211	75,000
Residential Interior Design	—	—	—	—
Landscape Architect	—	—	—	—
Civil Engineering	15,197	25,329	151,974	192,500
Structural Engineer	23,487	39,145	234,868	297,500
Mechanical Engineer	4,145	6,908	41,447	52,500
Security/Teledata Systems	—	—	—	—
Geotechnical Engineer	13,816	23,026	138,158	175,000
Subtotal Architectural/Engineering	**72,039**	**120,066**	**720,395**	**912,500**
Construction:				
Excavation/Foundation	315,789	526,316	3,157,895	4,000,000
Hollow Metal/Hardware	27,237	45,395	272,368	345,000
Roll Down Gate	—	—	—	—
Skylights	—	—	—	—
Curtainwall	—	—	—	—
Drywall	—	—	—	—
Tile/Stone	—	—	—	—
Wood Flooring	—	—	—	—
Carpet	—	—	—	—

Painting	—	—	—	—
Fire Extinguishers	—	—	—	—
Toilet Accessories	—	—	—	—
Window Washing Equip.	—	—	—	—
Appliances	—	—	—	—
Kitchen Cabinets	—	—	—	—
Window Treatments	—	—	—	—
Pools	—	—	—	—
Elevators	—	—	—	—
Plumbing	41,447	69,079	414,474	525,000
HVAC	29,605	49,342	296,053	375,000
Electrical	41,447	69,079	414,474	525,000
Subtotal Construction	**455,526**	**759,211**	**4,555,263**	**5,770,000**
Capitalized Taxes and Insurance:				
Real Estate Taxes	21,908	36,513	219,079	277,500
Insurance	3,553	5,921	35,526	45,000
Subtotal Capitalized Taxes and Insurance	**25,461**	**42,434**	**254,605**	**322,500**
Financing:				
Interest Cost	63,158	105,263	631,579	800,000
Loan Closing Costs	51,316	85,526	513,158	650,000
Suntotal Financing	**114,474**	**190,789**	**1,144,737**	**1,450,000**
Capitalized Leasing:				
Retail Space Planning	100,000	—	—	100,000
Sales Center	—	—	200,000	200,000
Building Model	—	—	250,000	250,000
Creative Direction	9,474	15,789	94,737	120,000
Collateral Materials	6,316	10,526	63,158	80,000
Subtotal Leasing	**115,789**	**26,316**	**607,895**	**750,000**
Capitalized General & Administrative	**128,289**	**213,816**	**1,282,895**	**1,625,000**
Contingency	**94,737**	**157,895**	**947,368**	**1,200,000**
SUBTOTAL BUDGETED—Capitalized Costs	**2,190,526**	**3,484,211**	**21,355,263**	**27,030,000**

Assume that after one full year, the project management team still believes the original budget is a reasonable estimate of the total cost of the project. Also assume that 20 out of the 30 condominium units have been sold. Therefore, based on the actual costs at this time, the project is deemed to be 32 percent complete. This percentage is determined by dividing the total capitalized cost incurred on the condominium portion by the capitalizable total budgeted cost of the condominium portion; thus, $21,355,263/$66,525,000 = 32%.

Exhibit 15.4 shows the 20 condominium units sold at this point.

Since $84,240,000 worth of the units has been sold, if this is the entity's year-end for financial reporting purposes, the project will recognize this revenue and profit:

Exhibit 15.4   Breakdown of Units Sold One Year after Start of Construction

Unit No.	No. Bedrooms	Unit Size	Sales Prices
1	2	1,600	$ 3,200,000
2	2	1,600	$ 3,200,000
3	1	1,300	$ 2,600,000
4	3	2,300	$ 4,600,000
5	4	2,800	$ 5,600,000
6	2	1,600	$ 3,200,000
7	2	1,600	$ 3,200,000
8	1	1,300	$ 2,600,000
9	1	1,300	$ 2,600,000
10	4	2,800	$ 5,600,000
11	2	1,600	$ 3,200,000
12	4	2,800	$ 5,600,000
13	3	2,300	$ 4,600,000
14	4	2,800	$ 5,600,000
15	4	2,800	$ 5,600,000
16	2	1,600	$ 3,200,000
17	2	1,600	$ 3,200,000
18	2	1,600	$ 3,200,000
19	1	1,300	$ 2,600,000
20	4	3,000	$ 6,000,000
			$ 79,200,000

Total units sold at year-end	$ 79,200,000
Percentage complete	32%
Revenue to be recognized	$ 25,344,000

The revenue recognized of $25,344,000 is determined by multiplying the percentage complete by the total dollar value of the units under contract (sold).

Note that as capitalized costs are incurred during the construction period, the required journal entry would be a debit to WIP and a credit to accounts payable or cash, depending when these costs are paid.

In the example, since at year-end we incurred total costs of $27,030,000 of which $21,355,263 relates to the condominium portion, the entries to recognize the revenue and cost of sales would be:

Receivable from buyers	$ 25,344,000	
Sales		$ 25,344,000
Cost of sales	$ 21,355,263	
Work in progress		$ 21,355,263

In most condominium projects, the developer collects deposits from the buyer when the contracts are signed. These deposits are recorded as liabilities in the developer's books. Assume that the total deposits on the 20 units already sold equal $20 million. The journal entry that would be recorded is:

```
Cash . . . . . . . . . . . . . . . . . . $20,000,000
Buyer Deposit Liability . . . . . . . . .   $20,000,000
```

Subsequent Periods

As this project is ongoing, actual costs incurred might be quite different from what was originally budgeted. Therefore, the original budget would need to be revisited and updated to reflect the current estimate of the total project cost. Note that updating the budget will affect the percentage complete of the project and therefore the revenue recognized.

Let us now go further and assume that during the first quarter of year 2, three new units were sold and $2,650,000 additional costs were incurred of which $1,650,000 relates to the condominium section. In addition, the construction budget is projected to increase by an additional $2,000,000 due to rising costs of construction materials that were not anticipated when the original budget was prepared. Of the total $2,000,000 cost increase, $1,578,948 will be spent on the condominium portion; the rest will be spent on the retail and parking garage sections. The updated budget is shown in Exhibit 15.5.

Exhibit 15.5   Sample Development Project Updated Budget, Year 2

Cost Categories	Parking	Retail	Condominium	Total
Site Costs	1,184,211	1,973,684	11,842,105	15,000,000
Architectual/Engineering:				
Interior Design	—	—	450,000	450,000
Design Architect	39,474	65,789	394,737	500,000
Production Architect	23,684	39,474	236,842	300,000
Surveying	5,921	9,868	59,211	75,000
Residential Interior Design	15,789	26,316	157,895	200,000
Landscape Architect	11,842	19,737	118,421	150,000
Civil Engineering	27,632	46,053	276,316	350,000
Structural Engineer	27,632	46,053	276,316	350,000
Mechanical Engineer	27,632	46,053	276,316	350,000
Security/Teledata Systems	27,632	46,053	276,316	350,000
Geotechnical Engineer	13,816	23,026	138,158	175,000
Subtotal Architectural/Engineering	**221,053**	**368,421**	**2,660,526**	**3,250,000**
Construction:				
Excavation/Foundation	505,263	842,105	5,052,632	6,400,000
Hollow Metal/Hardware	181,579	302,632	1,815,789	2,300,000
Roll Down Gate	1,579	2,632	15,789	20,000

(*continued*)

Exhibit 15.5   (Continued)

Cost Categories	Parking	Retail	Condominium	Total
Skylights	—	—	350,000	350,000
Curtainwall	—	—	4,500,000	4,500,000
Drywall	276,316	460,526	2,763,158	3,500,000
Tile/Stone	161,842	269,737	1,618,421	2,050,000
Wood Flooring	—	10,000	1,490,000	1,500,000
Carpet	—	—	750,000	750,000
Painting	94,737	157,895	947,368	1,200,000
Fire Extinguishers	5,921	9,868	59,211	75,000
Toilet Accessories	35,526	59,211	355,263	450,000
Window Washing Equip.	—	33,553	221,447	255,000
Appliances	197,368	328,947	1,973,684	2,500,000
Kitchen Cabinets	—	—	2,600,000	2,600,000
Window Treatments	—	—	200,000	200,000
Pools	—	—	1,850,000	1,850,000
Elevators	—	—	2,650,000	2,650,000
Plumbing	276,316	460,526	2,763,158	3,500,000
HVAC	197,368	328,947	1,973,684	2,500,000
Electrical	276,316	460,526	2,763,158	3,500,000
Subtotal Construction	**2,210,132**	**3,727,105**	**36,712,763**	**42,650,000**
Capitalized Taxes and Insurance:				
Real Estate Taxes	146,053	243,421	1,460,526	1,850,000
Insurance	23,684	39,474	236,842	300,000
Subtotal Capitalized Taxes and Insurance	**169,737**	**282,895**	**1,697,368**	**2,150,000**
Financing:				
Interest Cost	252,632	421,053	2,526,316	3,200,000
Loan Closing Costs	51,316	85,526	513,158	650,000
Subtotal Financing	**303,947**	**506,579**	**3,039,474**	**3,850,000**
Capitalized Leasing:				
Retail Space Planning	150,000	—	—	150,000
Sales Center	—	—	200,000	200,000
Building Model	—	—	318,816	318,816
Creative Direction	11,842	19,737	118,421	150,000
Collateral Materials	6,711	11,184	67,105	85,000
Subtotal Leasing	**168,553**	**30,921**	**704,342**	**903,816**
Capitalized General & Administrative	**513,158**	**855,263**	**5,131,579**	**6,500,000**
Contingency	**631,579**	**1,052,632**	**6,315,789**	**8,000,000**
SUBTOTAL BUDGETED—Capitalized Costs	**5,402,368**	**8,797,500**	**68,103,948**	**82,303,816**
Marketing—Expensed Component				
Retail Commissions	—	800,000	—	800,000
Condominium Closing Costs	—	—	1,000,000	1,000,000

Residential Marketing	—	—	250,000	250,000
Marketing Consulting Fees	—	—	120,000	120,000
Public Relations	—	—	100,000	100,000
Creative Direction	3,947	6,579	39,474	50,000
Subtotal Marketing—Expensed Component	**3,947**	**806,579**	**1,509,474**	**2,320,000**
Expensed General & Administrative	**9,474**	**15,789**	**94,737**	**120,000**
Income Taxes	**—**	**—**	**169,806**	**169,806**
Misc Income	**(229,902)**	**(383,169)**	**(2,299,017)**	**(2,912,088)**
TOTAL PROJECT BUDGET	**5,185,888**	**9,236,699**	**67,578,947**	**82,001,534**

At the end of this quarter, the percentage complete and revenue to be recognized would be determined as:

Prior-Period Condo Actual Cost	$ 21,355,263
Additional Condo Costs during the Quarter	$ 1,650,000
Total Condo Costs Incurred	$ 23,005,263
Percentage Complete	34%

The percentage complete is calculated by dividing $23,005,263 by $68,103,948.

The revenue to be recorded during this quarter would therefore be determined as:

Prior-Period Condo Sales (20 units)	$ 79,200,000	
3 Additional Units Sold	$ 12,000,000	
Total Condo Sold thru This Quarter	$ 91,200,000	
Total Condo Sold thru This Quarter	$ 91,200,000	
Percentage Complete	34%	
Total Sales since Inception	$ 31,008,000	(a)
Total Sale in Prior Period	$ 25,344,000	(b)
Sales for the Quarter	$ 5,664,000	(a+b)

The journal entries to recognize the additional revenues and costs for the quarter would be:

Receivables from Buyers	$ 5,664,000	
Sales Revenue		$ 5,664,000
Cost of Sales	$ 1,650,000	
Work in Progress		$ 1,650,000

COST RECOVERY METHOD

The cost recovery method is another method of profit recognition of real estate sale. This method can be used in either of these situations:

- Real estate transactions where the initial investment criteria were not met and the cost of the property cannot be recovered in the event the buyer defaults.

- Transaction where the unpaid balance of the sales price due to the seller from the buyer is subject to future subordination. A seller's receivable is subject to subordination if it is being placed in a position lower than another party's claim against the buyer.

The cost recovery method is also appropriate in transactions where the installment method is allowed; thus, either method can be used in a transaction that meets the criteria mentioned earlier under the "Installment Method."

Under the cost recovery method, no profit is recognized by the seller until the total payments by the buyer to the seller are sufficient to cover the seller's cost basis on the property.

On the seller's financial statements for the transaction period, the income statement should show the sales, the deferred gross profit, and the cost of the property sold; the balance sheet should show the receivables from the buyer net of the deferred gross profit.

Example

A property was sold for $1 million with a cost basis to the seller of $700,000 that qualifies to be accounted for under the cost recovery method. The journal entries at the time of sale would be:

Receivable from Buyer	$ 1,000,000	
Deferred Gross Profit (contra to sales)	$ 300,000	
Sales		$1,000,000
Deferred Assets (contrs to receivables)		$ 300,000
Cost of Sales	$ 700,000	
Property		$ 700,000

The seller's income statement will present the transaction as:

Sales	$ 1,000,000
Deferred Gross Profit	$ (300,000)
Net Sales	$ 700,000
Cost of Sales	$ (700,000)
Net Income	$ —

The seller's balance sheet would show:

Receivable from Buyer	$ 1,000,000
Deferred Assets	$ (300,000)
Total Assets	$ 700,000

Therefore, future periodic payments made by the buyer will be re-corded as a reduction of the receivables with a portion credited to interest income.

16

AUDITS

As this book has shown, there are numerous participants in the real estate industry, and the stakes are almost always very high. Real estate requires relatively huge capital, and most times that capital comes from numerous sources. For capital to flow throughout the industry, there has to be trust among the market participants and a system of checks and balances. Audits help provide this comfort and assurance.

In this chapter we discuss auditing: what it means, who performs audits, and how they are performed. In addition, we discuss the types of audits and their users.

"Auditing" has been defined by the American Accounting Association as "a systematic process of objectively obtaining and evaluating evidence regarding assertions about economic actions and events to ascertain the degree of correspondence between those assertions and established criteria and communicating the results to interested users."[1] This definition has been the most widely used. It is the most comprehensive definition of auditing, regardless of the type and nature of audit.

AUDIT OVERVIEW

In performing an audit, the auditor tests management's assertions regarding the financial statements. According to the Statement of Auditing Standards (SAS) 31, *Evidential Matter*, these assertions are:

- Existence or occurrence

- Completeness

---

1. American Accounting Association, "Report of the Committee on Basic Auditing Concepts," *Accounting Review* 47 (Sarasota, FL, 1973).

- Rights and obligations
- Valuation or allocation
- Presentation and disclosure

It is important to fully understand the meaning of these management assertions. In their book, *Modern Auditing*, Boynton and Kell define the terms in this way:

Existence or occurrence:
Assertions about existence or occurrence deal with whether assets or liabilities of the entity exist at a given date and whether recorded transactions have occurred during a given period.
Completeness:
Assertions about completeness deal with whether all transactions and accounts that should be presented in the financial statements are so included.
Rights and obligations:
Assertions about rights and obligations deal with whether assets are the rights of the entity and liabilities are the obligations of the entity at a given date.
Valuation or allocation:
Assertions about valuation or allocation deal with whether asset, liability, revenue, and expense components have been included in the financial statements at appropriate amounts.
Presentation and disclosure:
Assertions about presentation and disclosure deal with whether particular components of the financial statements are properly classified, described, and disclosed.[2]

Numerous audit firms can provide financial statements audits in the real estate industry. The four largest ones, popularly referred to as the "Big Four," are PricewaterhouseCoopers, Deloitte, Ernst & Young, and KPMG. These firms have global real estate audit professionals and can serve both small, local real estate firms and larger global ones. At the end of an audit, the auditors usually issue an audit report that contains their audit opinion.

Users of Audit Reports

In general, audit reports issued by independent auditors are highly valued for their objectivity, despite recent questions regarding their reliability. Nevertheless, audits are not going away. The recent problems have caused increased regulation and monitoring of auditors.

---

2. William C. Boynton and Walter G. Kell, *Modern Auditing*, 6th ed. (New York: John Wiley & Sons, 1996).

The main users of the auditor reports are:

- Investors
- Lenders
- Regulators
- Suppliers
- Customers

These users need audited financial statements and auditors' reports for various reasons. Investors need the material to determine the performance and financial position of the audited company in order to make investment decisions. Lenders similarly use the material to determine whether to lend money to the company, to what extent, and also at what cost. The regulators use it, among other reasons, to ensure that adequate information is provided to investors in a timely manner. Suppliers and customers use such information to determine whether to do business with the company and to what extent.

Audit Procedures

Upon completion of an audit, auditors provide a report that expresses their opinion. For the auditors to be able to express this opinion with confidence, they need to perform certain audit tests on the management's assertions. This process of testing management's assertions is called audit procedure.

During audits, the typical audit procedures are:

- Vouching
- Confirming
- Inspecting
- Tracing
- Observing
- Reperforming
- Counting
- Inquiry
- Analytical testing

These audit procedures are not all used at once on all account balances. Auditors determine which of one or a combination of procedures is appropriate for each account or management assertion.

Major Account Balances and Specific Audit Procedures

This section discusses some account balances and common specific procedures performed by auditors.

Cash   Cash is one of the balance sheet items most susceptible to theft, misappropriation, and misrepresentation due to its very nature. Investors, lenders, industry analysts, and vendors pay close attention to it. In auditing cash, auditors want to ensure that the cash balance is not materially overstated on the balance sheet date. Auditors tests this balance through confirmation of the cash balance with the bank. Usually the company prepares a confirmation letter signed by the appropriate company officer. This letter is handed over to the auditor, who mails the confirmation letter to the bank. The bank is advised in the confirmation letter to mail the confirmation directly to the auditor.

   As part of cash audit testing, auditors also request the company's bank statements and cash reconciliations to ensure that transactions and cash balances were properly recorded.

Accounts Receivable   These could be receivables from base rent, tenants' pro rata share of operating expenses, and property taxes. Auditors want to make sure the amount on the balance sheet is not overstated. It is important for auditors to make sure that they are valid receivables and collectible. This account balance can be audited in several ways. Auditors can confirm the balances with the tenants, similar to the way cash is confirmed. Auditors can also review the lease agreement to determine the base rent and the tenants' pro rata operating expenses and property taxes. Auditors also verify these amounts by vouching the amounts to the supporting documents, such as invoices and subsequent cash receipts.

   As mentioned, auditors not only test to determine whether the receivables are valid; they also want to make sure the receivables are collectible. They obtain this assurance by asking management for old outstanding receivables and by reviewing the supporting documents. In addition, auditors inspect the list of tenants with receivables to ensure they are viable companies and not ones in financial difficulties.

Prepaid Expenses   As with other asset amounts on the balance sheet, auditors want to make sure that prepaid expenses, which are assets, are not overstated. Some examples of prepaid expenses include prepaid insurance, prepaid legal fees, and prepaid property taxes. Auditors audit these accounts by reperforming the company's calculation of the balances and also inspecting supporting invoices and payments.

Land and Building Improvements   If auditors are auditing land and building improvements during the year in which they were acquired, they would need to audit the validity of this amount by inspecting the purchase and sales agreement and the evidence of payment. During subsequent years, the building improvements should be carried on the balance sheet net of accumulated depreciation. Auditors would review the company's depreciation policy and also recalculate the depreciation schedule to ensure that the depreciation schedule follows company policy and that reported net book value is not materially misstated.

Accounts Payable and Accrued Liabilities   Accounts payable and accrued liabilities are audited for understatement. Auditors want to get reasonable assurance that liabilities are not more than the company has stated in the balance sheet. The four principal ways in which auditors test liabilities are:

1. Search for unrecorded liabilities

2. Detail test of recorded liabilities

3. Review of contracts

4. Inquiry

Search for Unrecorded Liabilities   During the search for unrecorded liabilities testing, auditors request at least two items from the company: (1) subsequent disbursements from the day after the balance sheet date through end of fieldwork, and (2) a detailed listing of accounts payable and accrued liabilities.

Since the auditors' test is to ensure that liabilities are recorded correctly and also recorded during the correct period, selections are made from subsequent disbursements. For selected disbursements, auditors request invoices supporting the disbursements. If the invoices show that the disbursements represent transactions during the period being audited, auditors would trace the invoices to the accounts payable and accrued liabilities listing. If they are not on the listing, that would represent error that would be noted as audit adjustments.

Detail Test of Recorded Liabilities   During the detail test of recorded liabilities, auditors obtain the list of accounts payable and accrued liabilities. Auditors select items from the list and request supporting information for those items to ensure that the amounts recorded are not understated.

Review of Contracts   The review of contracts is performed to ensure that the company's obligations as noted on agreements with third parties are properly recorded. For example, some lease agreements require that landlord is to provide funding for lease incentives. These are liabilities at the time the lease is signed, and they should be recorded as such. If the agreement is not reviewed properly, this type of liability may be missed or not recorded during the correct accounting period.

Inquiry   Inquiry is a very important audit procedure. It involves discussions with the client personnel to gain insight into the events and transactions that may affect the audit in general or specific aspects of the audit. Inquiry involves both past and on going events and transactions. During inquiry, auditors are better able to understand the nature of the transactions and are better able to determine the best way to perform the audit to ensure there is no material misstatement.

Loans Payable   Loans are usually audited through confirmation from lenders. The debt confirmation normally asks lenders to confirm the loan balance as of the balance sheet date, including any accrued interests and the loan interest rate. The confirmation is usually signed by the appropriate officer of the company and mailed directly by the auditor to the lender. Upon receipt of the confirmation, the lender is instructed to mail the confirmation directly to the auditor.

Revenue   Revenue is one of the accounts that is more susceptible to misstatement. The revenue reported by an entity is of interest to many financial statement users. Revenue is closely watched by investors, lenders, vendors, and analysts. To audit revenue, auditors can use a number of audit procedures, depending on the type of revenue.

For rental revenue, auditors would request a schedule of revenues recognized and lease agreements. They would then trace the revenue on the schedule to the lease agreements and the payment supports. Auditors may also perform analytical procedures by comparing the revenues for the period to revenues from prior periods that have been audited. For example, auditors could compare the revenues by tenants for the 12 months ended 12/31/10 to the audited revenues by tenants for the 12-month period ended 12/31/09. Auditors would then inquire through management and obtain supports for unusual variances. Unusual variances could be due to terminated leases, new leases, or rent step-ups. It would be the responsibility of management to provide auditors with explanations for any unusual variances.

Operating expenses recoveries and property tax recoveries are audited by obtaining the schedules supporting the amounts recognized as additional revenues by the landlord. The underlying numbers in the schedules should have been audited as part of the expenses audit. The next step would include the auditors making sure all tenants' pro-rata shares used in calculating the recoveries agree to the individual leases and also making sure that expenses are properly included or excluded in accordance with the respective lease agreements. In addition, auditors check the company's calculation of expense gross-ups, if any, by reperforming the calculation and tracing the inclusion of gross-up to the respective lease gross-up clause.

For percentage-of-completion revenues recognized on a development project that qualify for this method, auditors would request the revenue calculation and would reperform the calculation. Auditors would then make sure the project completion factor used in determining revenue is appropriate based on the percentage of the total project that is complete.

For revenue recognized from the sale of assets, auditors would request the purchase and sales agreement, including payment support. The payment would then be vouched to the bank statement for verification.

One of auditors' most important objectives during a revenue audit is ensuring that there is appropriate revenue recognition cut-off. Auditors test cut-offs by auditing revenues recognized near the period-end. Thus, for a company with a December 31 year-end, revenues recognized before and after December 31 are thoroughly detail tested.

Expenses   Regarding expenses, auditors want to ensure that the company's expenses are not materially misstated. Auditors audit expense by performing expense cut-offs similarly to the revenue cut-off already described. Auditors also request detailed listings of expenses and select some of the expense items to ensure that the amounts recorded are supported by the invoices and payments. Auditors may also perform analytical procedures by comparing current-year amounts to prior-period audited amounts to determine whether there are unusual variances that need further testing.

TYPES OF AUDITS

There are four common types of audits in the real estate industry:

1. Financial statement audits

2. Internal control audits

3. Sales and use tax audits

4. Tenant audits

Each serves a different purpose, and each is performed for different users, though the procedures can be similar in certain aspects.

Financial Statement Audit

Financial statement audits are required to be performed by an independent Certified Public Accountant (CPA). The CPA is required to express an opinion on the financial statements of the company. The opinion to be expressed usually is whether the company's financial statements are free of material misstatement. In performing the audit in the United States, the CPA is required to follow the generally accepted auditing standards (GAAS), which are the auditing standards generally accepted in the United States.

Financial Statement Audit Requests   During the course of the audit fieldwork, auditors request information to help them form opinions as to whether the financial statements are materially misstated. Auditors commonly request these items:

- Draft financial statements
- Trial balance
- General ledger
- Invoices
- Purchase orders
- Lease agreements
- Board minutes
- Bank statements
- Canceled checks
- Rent rolls
- Accounts receivable aging report
- Confirmations
- Payroll registers
- Vendor agreements
- Management fee calculation schedule
- Supporting schedules
- Account reconciliation
- Correspondence with customers

Internal Control Audit

Internal audit is defined by the Institute of Internal Auditors (IIA) as "an independent appraisal function established within an organization to examine and evaluate its activities as a service to the organization."[3]

An internal audit ensures that activities within an organization are carried out appropriately as directed by management. In essence, this audit ensures that specific procedures for performing various transactions and

---

3. Institute of Internal Auditors, *Statement of Responsibilities of Internal Auditing*, Codification of Standards for the Professional Practice of Internal Auditing (Altamonte Springs, FL, 1993).

activities follow management's directive. For example, internal audit determines whether:

- Purchases and cash disbursements are approved by appropriate personnel.
- Journal entries are posted by appropriate personnel.
- Bank reconciliations are performed periodically as specified by management and approved by the appropriate personnel.
- Proper approvals are obtained before bank accounts are opened.
- General ledger accounts are timely reconciled and timely approved.
- Critical supporting schedules are reconciled to the general ledger and timely approved.

These are just some of the questions that internal audit helps to answer. Internal auditors not only answer these questions; they also can advise management and recommend control activities necessary to ensure adequate control and oversight of the company's assets and liabilities.

Internal auditors usually are the organization's employees. However, due to many reasons, such as lack of expertise or limited number of staff, organizations also hire internal auditors from accounting firms that have professionals who specialize in this field.

Some common documents requested by internal auditors are:

- General ledgers
- Account reconciliations
- Invoices
- Cash disbursement register
- Bank statements
- Annual operating expenses reconciliation with copies of tenant billing
- Property taxes schedule with copies of tenant billing
- Certificates of insurance
- Lease agreements
- Rent rolls
- Accounts receivable aging report
- Vendor agreements
- Management fee calculation schedule

- Capital projects tracking schedule
- Approved annual plan

Sales and Use Tax Audit

State laws require vendors to charge customers sales taxes on goods and services purchased within the state. Vendors are therefore required to collect the taxes and remit them to the state. If a customer purchases goods for resale, vendors do not charge sales taxes if the customer has a tax-exempt certificate issued by that state. However, if that customer ends up consuming those goods instead of selling them, then that customer has to file and pay use taxes to the state. In addition, goods purchased for use in a capital improvement are not exempt from taxes. Sales and use tax audits therefore are conducted by the state to ensure that organizations pay their sales and use taxes.

Underpayment or nonpayment of sales and use taxes discovered by sales and use tax auditors are subject to penalties and interests.

Some common documents usually requested by sales and use tax auditors include:

- Copies of sales and use taxes forms filed
- Sales and use tax payments support
- General ledger
- Invoices
- Listing of capital improvement work performed
- Bank statements
- Cash disbursement register

Tenant Audits

Certain tenant leases require that tenants pay base rent in addition to their pro-rata share of operating expenses and property taxes.

When this type of arrangement exists, the lease would specify the types of costs that should or should not be included in operating expense and property taxes. In some of these cases, the parties may agree that the tenant has the right to audit the landlord's books and records to ensure that expenses are properly included or excluded. This right to audit the books and records of the landlord by the tenant is called audit right.

In a tenant audit, the tenant requesting the audit hires and pays for the auditor. Some leases specify that if the auditor finds any overbillings by the landlord, the landlord would be responsible for the audit fees or a portion thereof in addition to the overbilling. For this reason, it is important for landlords to make sure that the operating expenses and property taxes billed to the tenants are correct.

Some common documents usually requested by auditors during tenant audits include:

- Property tax bills
- Operating expenses reconciliation
- Invoices
- Canceled checks
- Bank statements
- Payroll records
- Depreciation and amortization schedules
- Vendor contracts
- Management agreements
- Operating expense ledger

Index